Nisha Oza in association with
King's Head Theatre presents

WORLD'S END

By James Corley

World's End was first performed at
the King's Head Theatre on
Tuesday 27 August 2019

WORLD'S END
By James Corley

Cast
In order of appearance
Ylli **Nikolaos Brahimllari**
Besnik **Mirlind Bega**
Ben **Tom Milligan**
Viv **Patricia Potter**

Creative Team
Director **Harry Mackrill**
Designer **Rachel Stone**
Lighting Designer **Jai Morjaria**
Sound Designer **Harry Linden Johnson**
Movement Director **Chi-San Howard**
Production Manager **Harry Fearnley Brown**
Stage Manager **Rebecca Medlock**
Assistant Director **Matt Strachan**
Assistant Producer **Lettice Cook**
Dramaturg **Jennifer Bakst**

Featuring original artwork by Memli Zhuri

The Producer and Company would like to thank the following individuals for their generous support: Stephen Hall, Jonathan Kent, Jonathan Levy, Phyllida Lloyd, Peter Murray and Pieter Toerien.

Special thanks to Daniele Lydon and Annie Brewer for their help with the production.

The Producer wishes to acknowledge financial support from Stage One, a registered charity that invests in new commercial productions. Stage One supports new UK theatre producers and productions, and is committed to securing the future of commercial theatre through educational and investment schemes.

CAST

NIKOLAOS BRAHIMLLARI (Ylli)

Theatre credits include: *The Curious Voyage* (Talk Is Free Theatre); *The Best For All* (White Bear); *The Author's Voice* (Rag Factory); *Pains of Youth* (Omnibus) and *The Sting* (Southwark Playhouse).

Television and radio credits include: *On Kosovo Field* (Tamasha/BBC Radio); *The Rook* (Lionsgate) and *Humans* (Channel 4).

Film credits include: *Dagenham* and *Yellow Jacket.*

MIRLIND BEGA (Besnik)

Mirlind trained at YewTree Youth Theatre and Bird College.

He is making his professional stage debut in *World's End.*

TOM MILLIGAN (Ben)

Tom trained at the Royal Conservatoire of Scotland.

Theatre credits include: *Harry Potter and the Cursed Child* (West End); *The Slaves of Solitude* (Hampstead Theatre) and *Our House* (Royal Conservatoire of Scotland).

Theatre and radio credits include: *Jack Ryan* (Amazon/Paramount) and *Doctor Who – Warlock's Cross* (Big Finish).

PATRICIA POTTER (Viv)

Patricia trained at LAMDA.

Theatre credits include: *Half Life* (Ustinov, Bath Theatre Royal); *The Colby Sisters of Pittsburgh Pennsylvania* (Tricycle Theatre) and *An Eligible Man* (New End Theatre).

Television credits include: *Absolutely Fabulous, Holby City, Brookside, New Tricks* and *Law & Order, The Fixer, Jam and Jerusalem, Frankie, Doctors, Man Down, DCI Banks, Extras, WPC 56, Trial and Retribution, The Bill* and *The Scarlet Pimpernel.*

Film credits include: *Patrick, Just Charlie, Bridgend, Bonobo, Red Lights* and *Shakespeare In Love.*

CREATIVE TEAM

JAMES CORLEY (Writer)

James trained as an actor at LAMDA. *World's End* is his first play.

Short film credits include: *The Yellow Room* and *The Scene.*

HARRY MACKRILL (Director)

Harry was Associate Director at Kiln Theatre (2018-19) and Resident Director at the Tricycle Theatre (2013 – 2015).

Theatre credits include: *Let Kilburn Shake* (Kiln Theatre) and *Boy With Beer* (King's Head Theatre).

As Associate Director: *Peter Gynt* (National Theatre/EIF); *Angels In America* (National Theatre) and *Handbagged* (West End/UK Tour/Roundhouse Theatre Washington).

RACHEL STONE (Designer)

Theatre credits include: *Apologia, Hand to God* (English Theatre Frankfurt); *Dessert, Stalking the Bogeyman, Upper Cut, Short and Stark* (Southwark Playhouse); *Calamity Jane* (Tring Park School of Performing Arts); *The Grinning Man* (Trafalgar Studios); *Boy With Beer* (King's Head Theatre); *Cabaret* (ACT Aberdeen); *That Face, Carousel* (Landor Theatre); *The Hospital at the Time of the Revolution* (Finborough Theatre) and *Company* (Pleasance Theatre).

As Associate Designer: *Disco Pigs* (Irish Repertory Theatre, New York) and *Handbagged* (UK Tour, Roundhouse Theatre Washington and 59E59 New York).

JAI MORJARIA (Lighting Designer)

Jai trained at RADA and won the 2016 Association of Lighting Designer's ETC Award.

Recent designs include: *I'll Take You To Mrs. Cole's* (Complicite); *Whitewash* (Soho Theatre); *Aesop's Fables* (Unicorn Theatre); *The Actor's Nightmare* (Park Theatre); *Mapping Brent* (Kiln Theatre); *Mary's Babies* (Jermyn Street Theatre); *Glory* (Duke's Theatre/Red Ladder); *Cuzco* (Theatre503); *The Hoes* (Hampstead Theatre); *Losing Venice* (Orange Tree Theatre);

King Lear, Lorna Doone (Exmoor National Park); *A Lie of the Mind* (Southwark Playhouse); *46 Beacon* (Trafalgar Studios with Rick Fisher); *Out There on Fried Meat Ridge Road* (White Bear Theatre/ Trafalgar Studios 2) and *Acorn* (Courtyard Theatre. OffWestEnd Award nomination for Best Lighting).

HARRY LINDEN JOHNSON (Sound Designer)

Harry trained at The Royal Central School of Speech and Drama.

Theatre credits include: *God of Carnage* (Bath Theatre Royal); *Br'er Cotton* (Theatre 503); *Babette's Feast* (Print Rooms Coronet); and *Boy With Beer* (King's Head Theatre).

As Associate: *Orlando* (Schaubühne); *Norma Jeane Baker of Troy* (The Shed) and *Home, I'm Darling* (Dorfman/Duke of York).

CHI-SAN HOWARD (Movement Director)

Chi-San trained at the Royal Central School of Speech and Drama.

Previous Movement Work for theatre includes: *Catching Comets* (Pleasance Edinburgh/Royal Exchange); *A Midsummer Night's Dream* (Oxford Playhouse); *Variations* (NT Connections, Dorfman Theatre); *The Curious Case of Benjamin Button* (Southwark Playhouse); *Let Kilburn Shake* (Kiln Theatre); *Skellig* (Nottingham Playhouse); *Under the Umbrella* (Belgrade Theatre/ Tamasha/Yellow Earth); *American Idiot* (Mountview); *Carmen the Gypsy* (Arcola Theatre/Touring); *Bury the Dead, Homos or Everyone in America, Adding Machine: A Musical* (Finborough Theatre); *Describe the Night* (Hampstead Theatre); *Parade* (Mountview); *Love and Money, Pornography* (ALRA); *In Event of Moone Disaster* (Theatre 503); *Tenderly* (New Wimbledon Theatre) and *Cosmic Scallies* (Royal Exchange/Graeae).

MATT STRACHAN (Assistant Director)

Theatre credits include: *Starved* (Hope Theatre); *Little by Little* (Etcetera Theatre); *In the Wake Of* (Lion and Unicorn Theatre) and *GAPS* (Katzpace).

As Assistant Director: *Rasputin Rocks* (Stockwell Playhouse).

Matt was shortlisted for the Young Vic Genesis Future Directors Award in 2018.

NISHA OZA (Producer)

Nisha has previously worked for Tamasha Theatre Company, Kiln Theatre and The National Theatre.

As Associate Producer: *Missing* (Tristan Bates Theatre).

As Producer (film): *The Yellow Room* (2018) and *The Scene* (2019).

A Letter from the Artistic Director

Hello! Welcome to the King's Head Theatre

I'm delighted to welcome Artistic Associate Harry Mackrill back to direct the world premiere of James Corley's *World's End*. This stunning debut, which explores the Kosovo war, single parenthood and sexuality, encapsulates the King's Head Theatre's commitment to staging new work and providing a platform for underrepresented voices. I cannot wait for you to see this tender, warm and beautiful love story.

The King's Head Theatre has always been a home for ambitious programming and exciting emerging artists. Last year 88,029 audience members saw a show of ours: 37,586 at our 110-seater home on Upper Street and 50,443 on tour. At our home in Islington we had 686 performances last year of 113 different shows.

But we couldn't do any of this without your support. If you're already a supporter of the theatre thank you so much. If not would you consider signing up? You can become a Friend for just £25 a year. Every Friend and Supporter, as well as all the wonderful audience members who donate money in our bucket, is vital to ensuring we remain accessible for generations to come.

Thank you, enjoy your stay and we hope to see you again soon.

Adam Spreadbury-Maher
Artistic Director

Support the King's Head Theatre

'In uncertain times, it's great to see one of the stalwarts of London's fringe going onwards and upwards'

Mark Gatiss

The **King's Head Theatre** is an ambitious, thriving producing house located in the heart of Islington. From the emerging companies and creatives, to the thousands of audience members we welcomed through our doors last year, people are at the heart of everything we do.

Famous for an unapologetically broad programme of work and an unwavering commitment to ethical employment on the fringe, the King's Head Theatre occupies a unique place in the capital's theatre ecology.

Each year, the King's Head Theatre needs to raise £100,000 to keep producing and presenting ambitious work that supports, develops and values our artists, staff, audiences and alumni. We hope you will join us on that journey by becoming one of our **Supporters**.

There are three ways to become a Supporter:

Online   www.kingsheadtheatre.com/supporters
By Telephone   0207 7226 8561
In Person   at the box office

For further information or to discuss bespoke packages to suit you, please contact Alan on **friends@kingsheadtheatre.com**

KEY TO THE STAGE DOOR from £150 per year

Priority Booking Period
Exchange and reserve tickets at no extra cost
'KHT Insights email with production news and announcements ahead of the press
Invitations to Supporters Nights including private pre-show discussions
Acknowledgement in our published play texts and programmes
How this gift might help: £275 pays an actor's wages for one week

KEY TO THE DRESSING ROOM from £500 per year

All membership benefits offered with Key to the Stage Door plus:
Invitation to annual 'Behind the Scenes Breakfast' to hear the Artistic Director
share upcoming plans for the King's Head Theatre
Personal booking via the office
How this gift might help: £500 pays for all the costumes for one of our operas

KEY TO THE KING'S HEAD THEATRE from £1,000 per year

All membership benefits offered with Key to the Dressing Room plus:
Invitation once a year to breakfast with the Executive Director
Opportunity to book house seats to sold out shows
How this gift might help: £1,375 supports the Director for one production

ARTISTIC DIRECTOR'S CIRCLE from £2,500 per year

All membership benefits offered with Key to the King's Head Theatre plus:
Playtext signed by the company for each production attended
Invitation to lunch with the Artistic Director once a year
Opportunity to be given a backstage tour of the theatre for you and up to
5 guests finishing with drinks on the King's Head Theatre's stage
How this gift might help: £2,500 pays for the set design for one of our plays

AMBASSADOR from £5,000 per year

**An exclusive chance to be a truly integral part
of the life of the King's Head Theatre
All of the benefits of Artistic Director's Circle plus:**
Invitations to our Press Nights and post-show parties and the chance
to create additional bespoke benefits suited to your interests
How this gift might help: £5,775 pays for actors throughout the rehearsal period

The King's Head Theatre is a registered charity | Charity No: 1161483

King's Head Theatre Timeline

The King's Head Theatre is 48 years old, here are just a few of the highlights of our journey so far...

1970 — Dan Crawford founds the first pub theatre in London since Shakespeare's day and the King's Head Theatre is born.

1983 — A revival of *Mr Cinders*, starring Joanna Lumley, opens at the King's Head Theatre before transferring to the West End. It goes on to run for 527 performances.

1986 — Maureen Lipman stars in the Olivier Award nominated *Wonderful Town* at the King's Head Theatre.

1988 — Premier of Tom Stoppard's *Artist Descending a Staircase* opens at the King's Head Theatre before transferring to Broadway.

1991 — Steven Berkoff directs and stars in the UK premiere of *Kvetch* at the King's Head Theatre.

1992 — Trainee Resident Directors Scheme wins Royal Anniversary Trust Award.

2010 — Opera Up Close, founded by Adam Spreadbury-Maher and Robin Norton-Hale become resident company for 4 years.

2011 — *La bohème* wins the Olivier Award for Best New Opera Performance.

2015 — King's Head Theatre forms a new charity to secure the future of the theatre. *Trainspotting* is first performed at the King's Head Theatre – in August 2017 it hit it's 900th performance.

2016 — 43,857 audience members see a show at our London home - our highest footfall ever.

2017 — King's Head Theatre announces the transfer of *La bohème* & *Strangers in Between* to Trafalgar Studios 2 in London's West End. *La bohème* goes on to be nominated for Best New Opera Production at the Olivier Awards.

2019 — King's Head Theatre's production of Kevin Elyot's *Coming Clean* transfers to Trafalgar Studios 2 in London's West End.

2020 — King's Head Theatre moves to its new permanent home in Islington Square, securing the future of the venue for generations to come.

James Corley

WORLD'S END

A tragedy in many scenes

OBERON BOOKS
LONDON

WWW.OBERONBOOKS.COM

For Harry and Nisha

First published in 2019 by Oberon Books Ltd
521 Caledonian Road, London N7 9RH
Tel: +44 (0) 20 7607 3637 / Fax: +44 (0) 20 7607 3629
e-mail: info@oberonbooks.com
www.oberonbooks.com

PB ISBN: 9781786828187
E ISBN: 9781786828262

Cover image: Kate Harding
Cover design: Sam Mackrill

Printed and bound by 4EDGE Limited, Hockley, Essex, UK.
eBook conversion by Lapiz Digital Services, India.

Characters

BEN – Nineteen years old, British

VIV – Ben's mother, forty-nine years old, British

BESNIK – Nineteen years old, Kosovar Albanian

YLLI – Besnik's father, forty-three years old, Kosovar Albanian

Setting

The World's End estate, London

The action takes place from November 1998 to late August 1999.

Notes on the text

BEN has a stammer. Sometimes he repeats the initial consonant when speaking – trigger words being B, M and D; or he seizes up completely on the word, presented in the text like this (---), and either blurts it out or says something else instead.

// denotes an overlap in the text.

SCENE ONE

November 26ᵗʰ, 1998.

Around 3pm – the light is fading.

A walkway of a block of flats. High up. Two doors, number 11 and number 13, stand flanking each other. Cardboard boxes of various sizes laden with brown tape and felt tip scrawl block their entrances.

Out front is the River Thames, hinted at by the sound of seagulls.

YLLI, a strikingly present energy with dark features, is standing by the door to his flat (no. 11). He is wearing a thin dark suit.

YLLI: *(Calling.)* Besnik!

    Besnik!

BESNIK: *(From within, in English.)* What?

YLLI: *(In Albanian.)* What's all this?

BESNIK: What?

YLLI: What's all this rubbish out here?

BESNIK: I can't hear you, Dad.

YLLI: What you say?

BESNIK: I'm on the toilet!

    YLLI slams the door. He makes his way through the boxes before noticing a marble head on the floor.

    He picks it up and turns it over – checking if it's marble.

YLLI: *(In Albanian.)* Not bad.

    BEN enters unseen. BEN is a nervous presence who questions everything – including his own mind. He is holding a box with "Ben's machine" written on it. He stops at seeing YLLI. His posture lowers. He turns to walk back.

9

YLLI: Excuse me –

BEN: Oh hi –

There is a second of tension as the two lock eyes before YLLI laughs.

YLLI: This is all yours, huh?

BEN: Yes – it is – sorry –

YLLI: Forgive me – I'm sorry. I was just admiring –

YLLI puts the marble head down.

I forget – been empty for long time, you see. I'm used to no neighbour.

BEN: Oh I see...

YLLI: Here, Let me take for you –

BEN: Oh no it's OK –

YLLI: No no let me –

BEN: Honestly I can –

YLLI: *(Firmly.)* Please let me, ha?

BEN lets YLLI take the box from him.

YLLI: You have much more stuff?

BEN: Yes. Some more (---) bits.

YLLI: Really? My God. You have a family?

BEN doesn't understand.

YLLI: Or with friend? Girlfriend? Ah! *(Indicating the marble head.)* I see – real marble – lucky guy.

BEN: Oh no – that's not. It's me and my mum. My mum and I... are moving in – together.

YLLI: Mother son. I see. I see. *(Putting out his hand.)* Ylli.

BEN: *(Shaking it.)* Ben.

YLLI: Ben, huh?

BEN: Yeah. (---) Nice to meet you.

YLLI, still holding BEN's hand and looking at him intently.

YLLI: How old? I have son your age I think.

BEN: Nineteen?

YLLI: No way – same age! You two will be both friends, I think.

BEN: Oh. Maybe.

YLLI: His name is Besnik.

BEN: (---) Oh cool.

YLLI: Forgive me, Ben, but you look older.

BEN: Yeah I know. Always have. When I was six, people thought I was ten. It's because I'm a worrier. I worry (---) a lot. The lines *(pointing to his forehead)* that might be (---) why.

YLLI: You have a classical face, that's why.

BEN doesn't know what to do with that.

A moment. YLLI is still holding BEN's hand.

From the stairwell, VIV's voice, refined and unself-conscious, is heard.

VIV: Ben? Can you help? –

BEN: Oh – *(calling back)* coming –

VIV: I can't lift this on my own –

YLLI: Your mum. She needs help?

BEN: She's fine, I've got it – thanks –

VIV: Ben? Are you there?

BEN: *(Calling back.)* Yes –

YLLI: *(Walking to the stairwell.)* I go. The lift still not working, huh? Oh I know. It's crazy. Nearly a year now. *(Calling to VIV.)* I'm coming, don't worry *(To BEN.)* I tell the people downstairs, the head office or whatever, and every time they say they will fix – assholes, forgive me Ben – but it's been long time now.

BEN: Oh I see.

YLLI goes to rescue VIV. We hear voices "Oh are you sure?", "It's really heavy", "Bend from the knees" as BEN goes to the door of no. 13 and unlocks it. A shadowy interior greets him. He switches on the hall light – not working.

VIV appears – the opposite of what her voice conjured. Small with darting eyes, VIV works from a place of 'act now, think later'.

VIV: Not the day for the lift to be broken.

YLLI enters carrying a large oil portrait of VIV in her prime.

YLLI: I go complain for you.

VIV: Oh no don't worry. We're quite fit.

BEN: Mum?

YLLI: They never listen to me. Maybe they will listen to you, I don't know. They're bastards, to be honest with you.

VIV: That's the last heavy thing now. Thank you.

YLLI: *(Putting the painting down.)* It's OK.

VIV: So whereabouts are you then?

YLLI: Next to you. Number 11. We're neighbours.

VIV: Oh! And we've blocked you out!

BEN: Mum, the lights aren't working?

YLLI: *(Putting out his hand.)* Ylli.

VIV: Ylli? Ylli. French name.

YLLI: French? *(Laughs.)* No no. Albanian.

VIV can't compute this.

BEN: Mum?

VIV: Viv. Nice to meet you –

BEN: Mum!

VIV: Darling, have you met Illy?

YLLI: Ylli.

VIV: He's our neighbour.

BEN: I know.

YLLI: We met just now.

BEN: There's no light.

VIV: Just give me a second, Ben. *(To YLLI.)* Sorry – just did a four-hour drive from North Norfolk. Me in a van. *(Does a driving mime.)* Got lost coming into London. My usual way through the docklands got completely screwed because of the fucking Dome – closed my favourite road. Had to do a bit of improvising, OK, improvising. But we made it. Shit that reminds me, I need to put more money in the meter – Ben?

BEN: I'm sure you put enough in.

VIV: Can you check, darling?

13

BEN: Mum.

VIV: Here, take my bag – there's a tenner in their somewhere. You can get change from the shop.

BEN: What shop? Where do I go?

VIV: Just find one, sweetie, there'll be plenty.

YLLI: There is a Costcutter. Straight down and all the way round.

VIV: And if you get in a muddle, just ask someone.

Beat.

BEN reluctantly takes VIV's bag and goes.

YLLI: You're not from London?

VIV: Used to be. This was my village. Chelsea. The Kings Road. I know it well.

YLLI: So you're coming home.

VIV looks around the cold walkway. A gust of wind blows through, creating a howling sound. It's not the same.

VIV: Yes, in a way.

Beat.

VIV: Are you renting from Jenny too?

YLLI: Who?

VIV: Jenny? Wharton-Bailey?

YLLI: I rent from the council, yes.

VIV: Right. I see. Good. Well – Oh Ben! Why did you leave that there –

VIV goes and picks up the marble head.

14

YLLI: This is you?

VIV: Oh no!

YLLI: No?

VIV: No this is my great aunt Laura. She lived in Vienna, actually, Ylli. Jewish – very artistic – wanted to be a concert pianist.

YLLI: And did she?

VIV: Oh no. No – she never got the chance. Died of TB, apparently, very sad. It's all in the family history. Which is somewhere around here! Anyway, she's always looking over us.

YLLI: An artists' life is always a struggle.

VIV: Yes…

VIV places Aunt Laura on the floor.

VIV: Because Albania, that's near… where is that near?

YLLI: Kosovo. Kosovo is where I'm from.

VIV: Kosovo, that's *(realising)* oh – yes. We were just listening all about it on the news.

YLLI: Yes, the world is finally paying attention.

VIV: Oh it's just awful what's happening there, isn't it?

YLLI: It's a very bad time for my country. Has been for long time. Very bad.

VIV: I don't know why everyone can't just leave each other alone. It's horrible all this… bullying.

YLLI: It's worse than that Viv, believe me.

A moment.

YLLI: *(The painting.)* I move this in here.

VIV: Oh no, don't worry. My son can help me with that.

YLLI: No no – please. We are neighbours now.

VIV: You're not having to be somewhere?

YLLI: My work – but it can wait.

VIV: I don't want to get you in trouble.

YLLI picks up the painting. He sees it properly.

YLLI: Oh my – this is you!

VIV: A long time ago. We were all having portraits done back then – my friends – and… it's silly really. I look it now and I don't know who that is – anyway – it's followed me this far.

YLLI: But this is good – this is very good.

VIV: Do you think so? He went on to be very well known.

YLLI: It has the colour of your face, see.

VIV goes to look.

YLLI: Everyone has a colour – some people have dark – everyone has different colour face, Viv. Your face is light. And if I close my eyes – *(squinting his eyes looking at VIV)* I see where the brightness is. I see immediately what I am to do. When you capture the brightness, you capture the likeness. And this artist has captured your brightness. See?

VIV takes a quick look.

VIV: *(Not seeing.)* Oh yes. That's clever. Are you an artist?

YLLI: Of course. I don't look like one now – but I've done many portraits. Many portraits, Viv. And this style – is like mine.

VIV: I'd love to see some of your work.

YLLI: I don't paint so much now. No time. And people, they all prefer realism.

VIV: I wonder how Ben's getting on with the van.

VIV goes to look over the railing as YLLI continues.

YLLI: I don't like realism much myself to be honest with you. It's like photo. You see but you don't see. It's all very precise, the lines, but there is never any colour, any essence coming through. But in this painting I see all your colour. It's wonderful, I love it, to be honest with you.

YLLI rests the painting in VIV's hallway.

VIV: So what would you say your style is?

YLLI: Mine? The truth is I'm still searching for my style. Still searching, Viv!

VIV: I don't want you to be late for work.

YLLI: I will get my son to help. *(Shouting.)* Besnik! *(To VIV.)* One second, huh.

YLLI goes into his flat.

YLLI: Besnik!

VIV is left alone. She sits on one of the boxes. If she could have a cigarette now she would. She takes in the view of the Thames. She closes her eyes. The sound of the seagulls.

BESNIK appears. A neater, prettier presence than his father, his expression is thought through and clear. He has a gold ring in his left ear and is dressed head to toe in PUMA. YLLI pushes him out the door.

YLLI: Here. My son. Besnik.

VIV: Hello. Are you good at lifting?

YLLI: Oh my God – my son is always in the park lifting. Big arms.

BESNIK: Would you like these moved in?

VIV: Yes please!

BESNIK, with amazing efficiency, starts moving the boxes in.

YLLI: You'll be alright now Viv, yes?

VIV: Yes we'll be fine. Don't worry about me. I've moved plenty of times you know.

YLLI: Then we have much in common. *(To BESNIK, in Albanian.)* You stay till they're all in, understand?

BESNIK: *(In Albanian.)* Wipe your trousers Dad.

YLLI: *(In Albanian.)* What?

BESNIK: *(In Albanian.)* Your trousers.

YLLI sees the dust all over his trousers. YLLI laughs.

YLLI: *(Wiping himself down.)* My boy, always telling me what to do. Goodbye Viv. Welcome to World's End.

VIV: Thank you!

YLLI: *(Heading for the stairwell.)* And if any problem, please, just knock on our door, yes?

VIV: We will!

YLLI leaves.

A moment as VIV readjusts to this new presence.

VIV: Does he not need a coat where he's going?

BESNIK: Dad never wears coats.

VIV: But it's so cold.

BESNIK: I know. I don't understand. He's mental. If you need help by the way in getting your gas meter started, I can do that.

VIV: I just turn on the boiler don't I?

BESNIK: No it's on the meter.

VIV: You're kidding.

BESNIK: Did you not know?

VIV: No.

BESNIK: You fire it up with coins.

VIV: But all my change is gone in the van – sorry.

VIV is visibly distressed.

BESNIK: I've got some coins.

VIV: Oh no it's alright – I'll find a bank somewhere.

BESNIK: We keep a weekly supply. I'll give you a day's worth. Just pay me back once you're settled.

VIV: Are you sure?

BESNIK: Sure.

BESNIK goes to get change. BEN appears.

BEN: I got lost.

VIV: It's a bloody prepay meter.

BEN: What?

VIV: The gas, Ben, the heating.

BEN: What do you mean?

VIV: I mean we need money to get heat.

BEN: *(Not getting it.)* Yeah…

VIV: Why didn't Jenny mention this? I could kill her.

BEN: But you always pay for heating.

VIV: Not with coins. Did you get any change?

BEN: No I didn't know where I was going.

VIV: Ben.

BEN: Can you go?

VIV: It's fine. The boy next door is giving us some.

BEN: Who?

BESNIK appears with a giro bag of change. There is a moment when BESNIK and BEN both clock each other. They both pretend not to notice each other.

BESNIK: Here you go. This will get you started.

VIV: Thank you. I – this is such a pain, I'm sorry.

BESNIK: It's simple when you get the hang of it. And you actually save more money this way.

VIV: OK.

BESNIK: Do you want me to start it up for you?

BEN: We're fine –

VIV: If you wouldn't mind.

BESNIK: Sure.

BESNIK goes in.

BEN: Mum, what are you doing?

VIV: What?

BEN: We can do it ourselves.

VIV: Oh shut up, I'm not having you being neurotic right now.

BEN: But you should have known this would happen.

VIV: I didn't OK, Jenny didn't mention it, she – oh look can we please not argue –

BEN: This is just so crazy. And how are we going to fit everything in? There's one bedroom.

VIV: It's all I could afford.

BEN: In London.

VIV: Oh look, stop it.

BEN: And can you stop asking people to help. I can do it. We can do it *ourselves* –

Light comes on from within the flat. A warm glow.

BESNIK comes out.

BESNIK: It will warm up quickly. Ours is like a furnace.

VIV: Thank you so much.

BESNIK: No problem.

Beat. BESNIK looks to BEN, who is staring at the floor.

BESNIK: Let me know if you need any other help.

VIV: Will do.

As BESNIK is about to shut his door –

VIV: Do you like Nintendo?

BEN mouths "SHUT THE FUCK UP" to VIV. VIV ignores.

21

BESNIK: Sorry?

VIV: Nintendo. My son has a machine, a Nintendo. Are you into gaming?

BEN: Mum –

BESNIK: Oh nice. That's well good. What games have you got?

BEN: A few.

VIV: What's that game you got today, Ben, the new game. He's been going on about this game for weeks. We bought it on the way here. What's it called darling?

After a tense moment.

BEN: It's Zelda.

VIV: Zelda.

BESNIK: Zelda?

BEN: Zelda: The Ocarina of Time

VIV: Any clue?

BESNIK: Oh yeah, definitely. That game looks well good. Well good.

VIV: Maybe you two could play together?

BEN: It's a one-person game, but yeah sure.

A moment.

BEN: I'm just going to put this in.

BEN picks up the final box and heads into the flat. VIV smiles at BESNIK and goes in. BESNIK stays standing in the doorway. We see him have a moment.

BESNIK closes the door as the lights of the walkway flicker on.

SCENE TWO

Two weeks later.

Around 11pm.

Inside VIV's flat. The living area. Cramped. A sofa bed is pulled out.

BEN, in his boxer shorts and an I LOVE NY T-shirt, is sat behind VIV's desktop computer. He is signing into AOL dial up. BEN's face in the glow of the screen is one of serious intent. The Internet connects, a few clicks of the mouse, and then the sound of dramatic soap-opera-y music followed by –

PORN VOICE 1: *(In Russian.)* I just closed the deal. Am I good or what?

PORN VOICE 2: *(In Russian.)* You're a genius. I always knew that.

PORN VOICE 1: *(In Russian.)* Not just a genius, but a very good looking one.

Wet kissing sounds. BEN starts masturbating.

A knock on the door.

BEN stops and turns the volume down on the computer. He waits.

Another knock.

BEN pulls his boxers back up and moves away from the computer.

BESNIK: *(Through the letter box.)* Hello? It's Besnik from next door.

BEN doesn't know what to do.

BESNIK: Sorry to trouble you, but I misplaced my keys and was wondering if I can use my spare? Your mum took a spare, see.

BEN does a "For fuck's sake mum" action.

23

BESNIK: Hello?

I can see a shadow...

BEN has no choice. He opens the door.

BEN: Hello –

BESNIK: Did I wake you?

BEN: No, no, I'm up.

BESNIK: I was hoping you were in. Your mum works nights, right?

BEN: Yes.

BESNIK: Like my dad.

A pause. BEN doesn't know what to do.

BESNIK: So you cool to get the spare key?

BEN: Oh. Right. I – I hadn't (---) didn't know about this arrangement.

BESNIK: Oh right...

BEN: I guess I can look –

BESNIK: Cool.

BEN: OK. I mean I don't know where (---)

BESNIK: I can come in?

BEN: Um –

BESNIK: To help you look.

A moment, then BEN opens the door for BESNIK

BESNIK: It's well cold out there. It's going to snow tonight. Bet you anything.

BEN puts on the light. He sees BESNIK dressed up: leather jacket, black T-shirt, jeans and bright red trainers – all well fitted and perfect; except his lip, which is cut. BESNIK takes in the space.

BESNIK: You got the hang of the heating then.

BEN: Yes.

BESNIK: Well insulated these flats aren't they.

BEN: Yeah, it's really warm, um – thank you for the money. Has she paid you back yet?

BESNIK: Not yet.

BEN: Oh I'm sorry – she's –

BESNIK: It's OK. Don't worry about it. I'm glad you guys are settled in

BEN: Thanks.

A moment. BEN is unsure how to mention BESNIK's lip.

BESNIK: You alright?

BEN: Yeah, it's just your (---) face is…

BESNIK: *(Touching his mouth and seeing the blood.)* Oh – that's embarrassing – can I use your bathroom?

BEN: Yeah of course it's –

BESNIK: Back in a sec.

BESNIK goes to the bathroom. BEN is stunned into stillness, then quickly puts on his tracksuit bottoms by the computer. He makes the bed.

BEN: You OK?

BESNIK reappears holding a bit of toilet paper to his lip.

BESNIK: You got a cat!

BEN: Oh yes – Jane.

BESNIK: Jane?

BEN: Yeah.

BESNIK: Sorry – wasn't expecting Jane!

BEN: She's very friendly. She's deaf.

    Beat.

BESNIK: Any luck?

BEN: Key? No… this could be tricky –

BESNIK: Which area should I do?

BEN: No (---) don't worry about that, I'll (---) do it.

    BEN goes to the chest of drawers in the corner and starts to look through – chaos – papers fall down, no order.

BESNIK: I feel really bad!

BEN: It's fine!

BESNIK: I never lose anything.

BEN: Where do you think you saw them last?

BESNIK: They were in my coat pocket. Must have fallen out when I fell.

    BEN looks up.

BESNIK: Got in a fight on the bus. Friday night yobs.

    BEN doesn't know what to do with that.

BESNIK: They were just jealous of my shoes.

    Beat. BEN laughs nervously and carries on looking. BESNIK looks around.

BESNIK: I thought there would be two bedrooms.

BEN: Oh no. Just the one.

BESNIK: *(Referencing the sofa bed.)* Looks comfy though.

BEN: I don't plan on staying long.

BESNIK: You off to uni or something?

BEN: (---) Malaysia.

BESNIK: Where?

BEN: (---) It's in the Far East. *(Trying again.)* Malaysia.

BESNIK: Cool. You travelling or something?

BEN: No. My (---) dad lives there.

BESNIK: Wow.

BEN: Yeah. Been there for a long time. He's got another family and stuff. You know he's not (---). But I just think it would be cool to live out there for a bit, while I figure out what I want to do.

BESNIK: Malaysia.

BEN: Yeah. But not for a while though. It's just a plan. He has to OK it.

BESNIK: I see.

BEN: Yeah…

BESNIK: Did you know the guy who lived here before?

BEN: No.

BESNIK: No, no one did. He was a proper recluse, like, never went out. The only time he did was when he was brought out on a stretcher.

BEN: Oh no – did he…

BESNIK: Yeah. Heart attack. Like that. His heart like burst apparently.

BEN: That's awful.

BESNIK: *(Nonchalantly.)* It's how we're all going to go isn't it. The heart. Or cancer. Shall I take my shoes off?

BEN: No – you don't have to do that here.

BESNIK: Never know do you. With some families.

BEN: Why was he a recluse?

BESNIK: Who?

BEN: The guy?

BESNIK: I don't know. Some just are.

Beat. BEN worries about his future.

BESNIK: Let's forget about the key.

BEN: Oh no – no no – I can ring her. But I don't know where she's working tonight – it changes – the addresses (---) for now. She's only doing shift work until she get's something proper, something (---) solid.

BESNIK: It's OK. I appreciate you trying.

BESNIK heads to the door.

BEN: What time is your dad back?

BESNIK: Not for another few hours. I'll head over to his work. I'll wait for him.

BEN: *(Suddenly.)* I can make you a cup of tea?

BESNIK turns round.

BEN: If you… if you prefer to wait here?

BESNIK: OK. Cool.

BEN: *(Surprised at his hospitality.)* OK… cool. Do you take milk?

BESNIK: Whatever you have.

BEN: Right. Won't be a minute.

BEN goes to the kitchen. We hear the kettle boil and the usual sounds as BESNIK uncovers the remaining the areas of the room. On the shelf, he spots a singing fish. He presses play. The fish starts singing 'Don't Worry, Be Happy'. BESNIK takes off his shoes.

BEN comes in with two cups of tea.

BEN: Here we go.

BESNIK: Thank you. Tea.

A moment as they take their first sips.

BEN: Yeah – have a seat.

There is nowhere to sit apart from the sofa bed. A moment as they settle on it.

BEN: They're converse?

BESNIK: Yeah.

BEN: I haven't seen them in red.

Beat.

BESNIK: *(Pointing to the marble head.)* She a relative?

BEN: Supposedly. From a… different century.

BESNIK: You got a lot of stuff.

BEN: Yeah. We couldn't afford storage space so... Just family stuff, you know.

BESNIK: I'm not being funny, but have you thought about Antiques Roadshow?

BEN: No – she's chipped. We've moved around so often.

BESNIK: How often?

BEN: Um, *(counting on his hands)* eight?

BESNIK: Honestly?

BEN: Yeah. Mum likes change. But with our last place – in Norfolk – it was haunted, so...

BESNIK laughs.

BEN: But that's not why we moved, I mean. Really there was nothing for Mum up there and, and she wanted a change.

BESNIK: And what about you? Did you want a change?

Beat.

BESNIK: I've been to Norfolk.

BEN: Really? Whereabouts?

BESNIK: Can't remember. I was like fourteen at the time. I had this impromptu urge to see the sea. So I stole money from my dad's wallet and got the train up there. Found myself in this little seaside town. Wide sandy beach. I like the sea. It relaxes me. You get to see the sky. Not like here. Here there is always something in your eye line, spoiling it. Unless you're on the roof. I'll take you up the roof one day. That's cool.

BEN: Cool. Is it allowed? I'm up for it. But that's high.

BESNIK: Yeah, you don't go when it's windy.

BEN: No. I got stoned on a roof once. At school.

BESNIK: I don't like weed. Makes my heart go really fast.

BEN: No I don't like it. It wasn't my idea anyway, it was this guy called Toby – who was really hard to control, and he – *(catching himself)* sorry. Not important.

BESNIK: Go on, what happened?

BEN: Nothing.

BESNIK: You're quite posh, aren't you?

BEN looks uncomfortable.

BESNIK: Oh sorry, I didn't meant to be rude –

BEN: I'm not that posh.

BESNIK: You have a friend called Toby!

BEN: He wasn't a friend. He was a twat. He –

BEN sees BESNIK laughing.

BESNIK: I've upset you. I'm sorry.

BEN: *(Lying.)* No you haven't!

BESNIK: You can't be that posh. You wouldn't be here otherwise.

Beat.

BEN: So what are you wanting to do when…

BESNIK: When I grow up? I'm finishing my BTEC in accountancy.

BEN: Oh cool.

BESNIK: It's alright.

BEN: No it's it's (---) I wish I was good at maths.

BESNIK: No one wishes they were good at maths. Deep down, no one wishes that.

BEN: I guess.

The atmosphere hardens slightly.

BEN: My mum was saying your dad's an artist.

BESNIK: He's a security guard at Waterloo Station.

BEN: Oh.

BESNIK: But yes, he trained as an artist. Your mum's a nurse right?

BEN: A carer. At the moment. She looks after people who are about to die.

BESNIK: That's brave.

BEN: Yeah. She's had people die in her arms before.

Beat.

BESNIK: Thank you for the tea.

BEN: Mum's got whisky in the kitchen if you want –

BESNIK: I don't drink.

BEN: No I don't really drink much either.

Beat. They take some more sips.

BESNIK: So when are you going to get it out.

BEN: (---) Sorry?

BESNIK: I've been patient.

BEN: Um...

BESNIK: Because I know you've been on it. My room's just there you know.

BEN drops into a pit.

BESNIK: Come on! You can't have Mario Kart and not expect to play with people.

BEN: Oh right! Mario Kart – sure – uh…

BEN goes to set up his Nintendo 64

BESNIK: I have genuinely lost my keys though. That's no lie.

BEN: Yeah – I know!

BESNIK: What other games have you got?

BEN: Um… Mario World?

BESNIK: Had Mario on my Game Boy. Super // Mario Land –

BEN: Mario Land – me too. Um – Goldeneye?

BESNIK: Yawn.

BEN: And… and yeah and Zelda.

BESNIK: How far have you got?

BEN: I haven't started it yet

BESNIK: What! Why not?

BEN: I wanted to finish Mario World first.

BESNIK: You're telling me you've had the brand new Zelda game for two weeks and not played it? What's wrong with you?!

BEN: I just like to complete things before I start on a new thing.

BESNIK: Put it on.

BEN: Now?

BESNIK: Yes! I want to see Zelda in 3D. I've only ever played it on the Game Boy.

BEN: No – I want to wait.

BESNIK: It's not going to be any better if you wait.

BEN: But...

BESNIK sees his struggle.

BESNIK: Don't worry. I'm happy to watch.

BEN: No you can play as well.

BESNIK: No I want sit on the side and offer solutions.

BEN: OK.

BEN removes the sleeve of the Zelda game. He opens the box, carefully takes out the cartridge and slots it in the Nintendo 64.

BESNIK: Zelda is the princess right?

BEN: Right. And Link is the guy who has to rescue her. That's really the setup for all the Zelda games.

BESNIK: Always the same isn't it.

BEN: But there's so much more to it than that. We'll see, but there's a lot of psychology around the story this time. We'll see. That's what it says in the review anyway.

BESNIK: We'll see.

BEN: Yeah. *(Getting excited.)* I might just turn off the light – the reflection...

BESNIK: I'll do it

BEN switches the N64 on as BESNIK turns off the main light. The glow from the screen illuminates the two of them.

34

BEN: *(Serious.)* I'm going to press play now.

BESNIK: OK.

A moment.

BESNIK: Are you alright?

BEN: It's just... do you mind if we don't talk during the opening? The cut scenes are my favourite bit.

BESNIK: Mine too.

BEN presses start. Zelda's melancholy theme begins. The game has started.

SCENE THREE

January 5th, 1999.

Around 8am.

VIV's flat. The same. Faint classical music is heard playing from next door.

BEN is folding away his sofa bed. VIV appears from her bedroom, holding a phone bill. She is wearing a silk dressing gown and has curlers in her hair.

VIV: How is my phone bill nearly three hundred pounds?

BEN: What?

VIV: Look darling – look.

BEN: Why are you asking me?

VIV: You haven't been calling this 0898 number?

BEN: I don't use the phone.

VIV: Well then it's the Internet.

BEN: What? No.

VIV: Who have you been calling?

BEN: I haven't been calling anyone. I told you. I don't know what that's about.

VIV: Oh Jesus, I'm going to have to ring them –

BEN: No – don't do that –

VIV: Well there's a mistake, darling. I'm not paying this. This is crazy.

BEN: Let me see it –

VIV hands BEN the phone bill.

BEN: No – it's the Malaysia number.

VIV: This isn't international.

BEN: Yeah but they've changed their number. And I rang them a few times.

VIV: But they always ring you. *(Looking at the bill.)* No it can't be that, it can't be.

BEN: Are you sure?

VIV: I'm cancelling the Internet.

BEN: No!

VIV: Just until I find another job // please, darling!

BEN: That's so unfair –

VIV: Ben – with what money can I pay this?

BEN: It's not the Internet's fault. I mean you're always on the phone to your girlfriends.

VIV: No one gets through to me because you're always online. I knew I shouldn't have got it, but you were pushing me very hard. –

BEN: Mum!

VIV: I don't have the money, darling! I'm sorry. I'm in the red on all my accounts. The bank won't extend my overdraft any more –

BEN: Just calm down. We can pay this in instalments. Like we did with the vet. It's not the Internet. I promise you.

VIV: Well you ring BT and you find out what it is, OK?

BEN: Mum!

VIV: Please, Ben, just do it – I have a job interview…

VIV goes to her room.

BEN: I don't know why you're going.

VIV: *(Off.)* Oh stop it –

BEN: You already have a job.

VIV: *(Off.)* OK – would you rather me stay in care? Working all nights and getting no sleep? Or do you want me back in that place in Norfolk? Where I was getting bitten and hit and coming home with bruises all over – is that what you want?

BEN: I want you to stick to one thing, instead of (---) always changing your mind and leaving me to be your fucking housekeeper. I shouldn't have to be taking Jane to the vet and and and buying the food –

VIV comes back in, furious, wearing just her bra and skirt

VIV: Well you get a job then.

BEN: Oh my God.

VIV: I'm serious. If you want the Internet and all these things, you go out there and you bloody pay for them.

BEN: I've tried // to get a job

VIV: You tried for one afternoon. // You have to keep knocking on doors.

BEN: No – more than that. Oh shut up.

VIV: You can't just give up at the first hurdle. I don't know why you just don't go down to that school in the estate and hand in your CV.

BEN: Because I don't have any experience, Mum!

VIV: They'd love someone like you.

BEN: Oh my God. Just go to your interview!

VIV goes back to her room. BEN looks at the phone bill.

BEN: *(To himself.)* Fuck.

VIV comes back in, holding the rest of her outfit. She changes into it throughout the following:

VIV: Or what you could always do is phone your father.

BEN: Mum.

VIV: I mean does he have a clue where we are? Did you send him those photos?

BEN: No.

VIV: Why not?

BEN: Because it wouldn't make any difference.

VIV: But at least he would get the picture –

BEN: This was your idea to come to London. You knew it would be more expensive. I don't know why this all such a shock for you –

VIV: *(Letting go.)* I'm allowed to want to have a better life, Ben!

BEN: *(Meeting VIV's energy.)* I've done what you wanted me to do. I was there in court, wasn't I? Why do you always want more? I can't – it's not – he's not (---) oh fucking hell.

BEN goes to his Nintendo 64. He puts it on. VIV has finished changing.

VIV: OK, I'm sorry. *(Beat.)* I'm sorry you feel all this pressure darling. I don't want you to feel caught in the middle. I've tried really hard to avoid that. It's just that your father is such a difficult man. I've never // known –

BEN: Mum.

VIV takes a breath.

VIV: You're right. I won't mention him anymore. OK? From now on. Zipped. *(Lightly.)* Fuck him. Hmm? Fuck him. We don't need him to be OK, do we? We've got this far. And I'll find something. We'll stay afloat. We always do. My miracle boy.

VIV kisses BEN's head.

How far have you got in the game?

BEN: Not that far.

VIV: Fish and chips tonight?

BEN: *(Perking up.)* That'll be great.

VIV gets up. She presents herself to BEN.

VIV: What do you think? Can I get away with this top? The offices are in Piccadilly so…

BEN: Definitely. The black makes your eyes ping out.

VIV: And note – your lovely earrings.

BEN: I knew they'd look good on you.

VIV: Not too much for office manager?

BEN: No no. They're great. They're perfect. They're fun.

VIV: Great.

Beat. VIV has a nervous moment. She pinches at her outfit.

BEN: Are you alright?

VIV: Yes I'm fine darling. It's just the cat hair gets everywhere.

BEN: They'll love you.

VIV: (*Spraying herself with perfume and snapping out of her mood.*) We'll see. Now don't worry about anything, OK? You just veg out and play your game today.

BEN: Thanks Mum.

VIV kisses BEN on the face again. She takes the phone bill off him.

BEN: It was the Internet.

VIV: What?

BEN: It was my fault. I was downloading stuff off the Internet.

VIV: What sort of stuff?

BEN: …

A moment as BEN struggles to come up with a lie. VIV instinctively rescues him.

VIV: Doesn't matter. I don't need to know. Just promise me you won't do it again. OK?

BEN nods.

VIV: I've got to go.

BEN: Good luck.

VIV heads to the door.

VIV: There are turkey escalopes are in the freezer.

BEN: Oh Mum – money for the boiler?

VIV: Oh Christ –

BEN: You forgot.

VIV: I'm sorry, darling. Can you ask next door?

BEN: It doesn't matter.

VIV: No don't get cold. Just ask them. It's what people do. People ask for things all the time.

BEN: Bye Mum.

VIV: Love you.

VIV leaves. The sound of next door's classical music gets louder.

BEN puts on a game.

SCENE FOUR

A week later.

VIV's flat.

BEN is playing Zelda. BESNIK is watching.

BESNIK: OK, so let me get this straight.

BEN: Yeah.

BESNIK: You're Link.

BEN: That's right.

BESNIK: And you've just found out that you're an orphan.

BEN: Yes. The Great Duku Tree is not my father.

BESNIK: Well that makes sense.

BEN: I'm not an elf, but a human – a Hylian.

BESNIK: And that means –

BEN: I have to find out my destiny from Princess Zelda. But first I – we – need to get these three spiritual stones.

BESNIK: Got it.

BEN: Which I'm guessing will then give me the Ocarina of Time. Which will allow me to travel back and forth in time.

BESNIK: Yeah. It will be nice when you're an adult.

BEN: *(Not really understanding.)* ... yeah.

BESNIK: Where are you now?

BEN: Um – Hylian field?

BESNIK: Looks like Kosovo.

BEN: Does it?

BESNIK: When do you get the horse?

BEN: I'm not sure.

BESNIK: That'll save time, won't it.

BEN: Do you want a go?

BESNIK: No it's alright.

BEN: I've been hogging it for ages.

BESNIK: It's your game.

BEN: Maybe if I get the first spiritual stone, you can get the second? Or if I die, you have a go, and vice versa. Or –

BESNIK: I'll let you know when I want a go.

BEN encounters a foe. His face contorts in concentration.

BESNIK: You alright?

BEN: Yeah just killing that.

BESNIK: Well done.

BEN: Thanks.

BEN breathes out. BESNIK laughs.

BEN: What?

BESNIK: Nothing

The phone rings. BEN lets it.

BESNIK: You going to?

BEN: No.

The phone goes to answerphone.

VIV'S ANSWERPHONE GREETING: Hello, this is 241719. I'm sorry I can't get to the phone right now, but if you'd like to leave message, please do so after the beep. Many thanks.

BEN: That's our old number.

BEEP

VIV: *(Sound of a busy office.)* Ben? It's only me, darling, are you there? Hello? *(Pause.)* You're probably playing your game. Just seeing how you are, OK. Love you. Oh and can you make sure you do the cat litter tray? Please. It's not nice for her otherwise. I have to go. Love you. Bye.

(Throughout the rest of the scene, we hear the beep of the answerphone every 30 seconds. It beeps until the message is played.)

BESNIK: How's your mum finding her new job?

BEN: Yeah, loving it. She gets to boss people around, so…

BESNIK: Cool.

She's got nice diction, your mum.

BEN: Um – how's your dad?

BESNIK: He's working on his self-portrait.

BEN: Cool.

BESNIK: He wants your mum's opinion. I think he thinks she's an art expert or something.

BEN: Oh no – she's not.

BESNIK: She is now.

BESNIK: How old is Jane?

BEN: Thirteen

BESNIK: Yeah. That's old for a cat.

Do you think she'll ever come out of the bathroom?

BEN: *(Laughs.)* I hope so.

> *BESNIK, enjoying his triumph in making BEN laugh, lies down and stretches on the rug. His T-shirt rolls up, revealing his torso.*

BEN: *(Glancing over.)* You alright?

BESNIK: Yeah. Just my shoulders.

> *BESNIK carries on stretching on the rug. BEN tries to concentrate on the game.*

BESNIK: Do you do any training?

BEN: Like, in the gym?

BESNIK: Yeah or in the park. That's where I train.

BEN: Cool.

BESNIK: You've got big shoulders. They would pop if you did weights. Like Popeye –

> *BESNIK touches BEN's shoulder playfully. BEN flinches dramatically.*

BEN: Sorry.

BESNIK: You OK?

BEN: Yeah just got a sore – *(circles his shoulder.)*

BESNIK: You scared me!

BEN: Do you want a go?

BESNIK: You've not died yet.

BEN: No – go on.

BESNIK: No!

> *Beat. BEN carries on playing. The atmosphere has changed. BEN tries to cover it up.*

BEN: So where would you go if you could go back in time?

BESNIK: I wouldn't go back. I'd go forward. I can do that right? If I had the Ocarina of Time I can go back or forward?

BEN: Yeah.

BESNIK: Yeah, I'd go forward.

BEN: How far?

BESNIK: To when I'm twenty-five.

BEN: Twenty-five?

BESNIK: Yeah.

BEN: OK...

BESNIK: Think about it. I'll be an adult, but I'll still be young. I'll be living somewhere that isn't World's End. I'd have a job, a salary. A car. I'd be free to do what I want. Maybe even own a cat like Jane. It'll be cool to experience that. For like a week. Make my accountancy lessons go a bit quicker.

What about you?

BEN: Um... I'd go back.

BESNIK: How far?

BEN: To when it was easier.

BESNIK looks at BEN to elaborate, but BEN is too in the game to do that.

SCENE FIVE

January 15th, 1999.

Around 10pm.

YLLI's flat. Sparse. YLLI, drunk and in his security guard uniform, is sat watching news footage of the Raçak massacre in Kosovo. An easel and canvas is lying on the floor, along with used tissues and an empty bottle of whisky.

A door opens.

YLLI: Besnik? Is that you? Sit down and watch this with me. You see what they've done now – the fucking Serbs? They've just massacred a whole village in Kosovo. Raçak. They rounded up our people, chased them into the woods and shot them like wild animals. Forty-five people – killed. Women and children as well – see – butchered, in the woods, can you imagine? The US envoy just said it's a crime against humanity. Won't be long now. We will get the bastards.

BESNIK appears. He puts his bag down.

YLLI: How did it go?

BESNIK: Why aren't you at work?

YLLI: They got the money OK?

BESNIK: Dad –

YLLI: Tell me, Besnik, tell me. The money. Did you give them the money?

BESNIK: Yes, Dad, yes, I gave them the money.

YLLI: How much?

BESNIK: Three thousand.

YLLI: Three thousand! This will get them. The whole world is waking up. The KLA will kill every one of these bloodsucking murderers. And America will help us – mark my words.

BESNIK: I'm not doing it again.

YLLI: Did they hurt you?

BESNIK: I am not doing it again.

YLLI lights a cigarette.

YLLI: You want a drink, Besnik?

BESNIK: Twice is enough. They don't need any more of our money.

YLLI: Please join me, huh?

YLLI pours two whiskies. He hands one to BESNIK.

BESNIK: *(Not taking the drink.)* What happened, Dad.

YLLI: I wanted to finish my painting. But as you can see, it didn't go so well.

BESNIK: I'm not asking that, Dad. I'm asking why you're // not at work

YLLI: Dad, no no, you call me Papa, understand?

BESNIK starts picking up the used tissues.

YLLI: Fucked up myself. When I start – and then I did something – so I went to correct it – and then I smash it.

BESNIK: And your job?

YLLI: It was wonderful, Besnik. It was my mistake, it was my mistake. I went to do something – and I shouldn't have touched it – it was very nice – it was perfect –

BESNIK: Dad!

YLLI: *(In Albanian.)* Do not call me that. You call me Papa. You respect your papa. Understand me?

BESNIK: Yes, Papa.

YLLI: What you want to know? They're assholes. That's all you need to know. They fired me. The bastards fired me. Fucking hell, I am so angry.

BESNIK: Why?

YLLI: They say I'm not focused and that they could smell drink on my breath. How would they know? If they came that close to me, I would have punched them in the face, believe me, Besnik… assholes.

BESNIK: And were you?

YLLI: I had one glass *(lifts up the miniature glass)* one glass, as always, before I go.

BESNIK can't help but shake his head.

Please. You think I would drink on my job?

BESNIK: No. Not on purpose.

YLLI: They wanted rid of me – from the start. The other guys there. I heard one of them call me a terrorist. Can you imagine? Fucking bastards. It's not my problem if they can't accept me.

BESNIK: Well it is your problem now. It's both our problem. What are we going to do?

YLLI: I'm going to sell my painting.

BESNIK: Which one – this one? This one here?

BESNIK goes to pick up the canvas off the floor.

YLLI: Don't touch it! Leave it there. I can't see it now.

BESNIK stands waiting.

YLLI: I made a mistake on it, but I will get it back. It will be my best work, believe me. Sometimes you have to make a mistake for something better to come back.

BESNIK: So you sell your great masterpiece, and then what? That will stretch us to what – a couple of months? Then what?

YLLI: Then? Then I go get work on the street – Leicester Square – drawing tourists.

BESNIK: On the street, Papa! Come on –

YLLI: I have that friend – he's offered me a spot – I don't know why you don't believe me –

BESNIK: It won't be enough.

YLLI: I can stay all day and all night if I have to. I don't care –
at least I will be using my gift.

BESNIK: Oh my God, your gift. Look where your gift's got us!

YLLI: You don't understand how it is for me. How it is for an
artist, like myself, to do piece of shit job like that, standing
all day for six pounds an hour, telling people where the
fucking platform is. And for what? For my own son to
judge me?

BESNIK: I don't judge you for having a secure job. I judge you
for putting our lives at risk for your art and for your country.

YLLI: Well then you are a traitor. You would let our people,
our land be destroyed for your own comfort. You are not a
fighter. You will not go to heaven.

BESNIK: If Mama was alive, she would tell you you're wrong.

YLLI: That I'm wrong?! She was more worried about you. You
becoming the disgusting pig that you are now.

BESNIK: Stop talking now –

YLLI: You shaving your legs and arms, putting on make up –
dressing up in your mother's clothes! We knew all about it.
She told me to ignore, that you would grow out of it. But
no. This country has made you soft. Have you forgotten
what happened to us? It's my fault. I thought coming here
would save us – can you imagine? And now look. My wife
dead // my son a fag.

BESNIK: // That's enough Papa –

YLLI: We'd be better off slaughtered in our own village –

*BESNIK picks up the empty bottle, smashes the head off and puts
it to YLLI's throat.*

BESNIK: Stop, Papa, stop.

YLLI: Ah you haven't quite forgotten my son. That's good. Maybe you will survive after all.

A moment as BESNIK looks into his father's inebriated eyes.

YLLI: I miss her so much. You have no idea. The loneliness I feel. I don't know what to do Besnik. I'm lost.

BESNIK takes his bag and leaves.

YLLI: *(Laughing.)* Going to wet your whistle? You have your Papa's appetite. *(Pouring himself another and raising his glass.)* To my country: Gëzuar!

SCENE SIX

The next week.

VIV's flat.

BESNIK playing, BEN watching.

BESNIK: I got a Game Boy when I came here. I was eleven. When we got off the plane we were all put in this leisure centre in Saffron Waldon. Me, Mum and Dad slept together in this sports hall – we had to until we were housed. And sometimes locals would drop in and give us clothes and stuff. Give us tea. And then one day this old lady came in, and instead of giving me clothes she gave me a Game Boy. It must have belonged to one of her grandkids or something because it wasn't new. Everyone was crying and missing home, but I was having a great time playing Super Mario Land. My only goal was getting to the end of each level. Got to get to the end of each level! I would stay up all night, playing it under my covers. And then once I finished that game, my dad took it away and that was it. No more consoles.

Man I'm loving this horse.

BEN: It's cool isn't it!

BESNIK: You see – it's so much better being adult Link.

BEN: Oh yeah yeah yeah – definitely.

BEN: Where are you going?

BESNIK: I don't know. Just riding.

BEN: Yeah…

> That's what's good about this game, isn't it. You can just go anywhere you want. It's so (---) clever, isn't it?

BESNIK: It is that.

> *BESNIK smiles.*

BEN: What?

BESNIK: Nothing.

BEN: What?

BESNIK: Where's the most exciting place you've been?

BEN: …

BESNIK: And it can't be your bedroom, HMV or the cinema.

BEN: I hate this game.

BESNIK: One place.

BEN: I haven't been there yet.

Is that bad?

BESNIK: No.

BEN: It's not?

BESNIK: Why is everything either good or bad with you?
You're like my dad.

BEN looks concerned.

That scared you!

BEN: No – I

BESNIK: Don't worry. You got time to change.

BEN: So are you like your mum then?

Beat. BESNIK looks uncomfortable.

Sorry.

BESNIK: I'm just myself.

The phone rings.

BESNIK: You gonna…?

BEN: No.

VIV'S ANSWERPHONE GREETING: Hello, this is 241719.
I'm sorry I can't get to the phone right now, but if you'd
like to leave message, please do so after the beep. Many
thanks.

BEEP

VIV: Hello darling, it's only me. Just wondering how you are
and how it's all going. Uh tonight, sweetheart, I won't be
back till late as I'm being taken out for dinner, actually,
which is nice, um, with Philip. You remember me talking

54

about Philip. Philip from work? Well anyhow there are those fish in a bags in the freezer, so what I would do is cook up a load of rice and –

BEN turns the answering machine off.

BEN: Sorry. It's distracting.

BESNIK: Your mum's getting lucky then!

BEN sits back down as if nothing's happened.

BESNIK: So what else can we do as adult Link?

BEN: Um…

BESNIK: Can we drink alcohol?

BEN: Um – maybe we could – let's go to Hyrule town and see.

BESNIK: Or smoke?

BEN: No.

BESNIK: Have sex?

A moment. BEN is caught in his mouth.

BEN: Uh (---)

BESNIK: We can't do that in Hyrule town?

Take that as a no.

BEN: We can fish?

BESNIK: So he's not really an adult, is he? It's still a kids' game.

BEN: No it's not a kids' game.

BESNIK looks at him.

I mean kids can play it, yeah, but adults can as well. I mean they're never going to show sex in a video game, are they?

BESNIK: They show violence.

BEN: That's different.

BESNIK: Have you not played Resident Evil?

BEN: Not my type of game.

BESNIK: But it's messed up, right. Going into houses and shooting people.

BEN: Zombies.

BESNIK: Who were once people.

BEN: Yeah but they can't show Link having sex!

BESNIK: But he's of age. He can do what he wants. Why are the game designers limiting him? Why are they limiting us?

BEN: We're not being limited –

BESNIK: He doesn't even have a job. He's just wandering around, saying nothing –

BEN: *(Getting fired up.)* What are you talking about – he has a quest to complete! He has to free the six sages, find Zelda and then somehow destroy Ganondorf. I mean there's no time for anything else.

BESNIK: Nintendo's for kids.

BEN: *(Meaning it.)* Nintendo is not for kids.

BESNIK: Yeah it is. It's Disney. It's not real.

BEN: It's not anything to do with Disney. It's Japanese.

BESNIK: Playstation. Now that's an adults' console.

BEN: Playstation's shit.

BESNIK: *(Surprised.)* OK.

BEN: All their games are rubbish. You can't play them – I
   tried – and they're all lazy and and (---) macho and not
   beautiful.

   *Beat. BEN feel's like he's said too much. BESNIK hands him the
   controller.*

BESNIK: OK.

BEN: It's my go?

BESNIK: I died.

BEN: Oh.

   BEN takes the controller back. He plays.

BESNIK: Macho and not beautiful. I like that.

BEN: I was just saying crap.

BESNIK: You know I'm team Nintendo, right?

   BEN nods.

BESNIK: All the way.

SCENE SEVEN

February 13th, 1999.

YLLI's flat. Evening.

An effort has been made – red tablecloth, bowl of cookies and Classic FM is on in the corner (it's Mozart hour) – but still the overwhelming effect is sparse. The television, with no sound, is on.

VIV, tired but making an effort, and BEN, holding a box of Guylian chocolates, have just walked in. BESNIK sits by as YLLI plays host.

YLLI: Welcome! Come in, come in, come in –

VIV: Thank you – oh! Yours is different to ours.

YLLI: Our flat? You think so?

VIV: Oh yes – it is. Is that another bedroom?

YLLI: We have two bedroom. You not have two?

VIV: No. May I have a look?

> *VIV charges in to look anyway.*

YLLI: Of course, just wait one second, Viv. I show you –

> *YLLI follows her. We hear them talk about the spare room and the bathroom that makes the same loud noise when you flush the toilet during BEN and BESNIK's interchange.*

BESNIK: Sorry in advance

BEN: What for?

BESNIK: For Dad. And the food.

BEN: Smells nice. *(Handing over the chocolates.)* For you guys.

BESNIK: Thanks. Oh – seashells. Classy.

BEN: They're Belgium (---) Belge

BESNIK: You look different.

BEN: Do I?

BESNIK: It's seeing you in another environment. It's weird.

BEN: You got your ear pierced.

BESNIK: Yeah. Again. *(Showing BEN the two hoops in his left ear.)* Two.

BEN: What does that mean?

BESNIK: That I'm cool.

VIV and YLLI reappear.

VIV: No we don't rent through the council.

YLLI: Ah. Yes. I remember you say.

VIV: Private landlord. Jenny?

YLLI: Not a very good one, I think.

BEN: No.

VIV: She's been very good to us over the years. And we go back a long time. Friend of my first husband's.

YLLI: You've had many husbands?

VIV: Two. But if I'd known how bad the second was going to be, I'd have never divorced the first! Were you married?

YLLI: Yes, a long time. But she died.

VIV: Oh no.

YLLI: Cancer, Viv. Very bad.

BESNIK: Can I get you anything to drink, Viv?

VIV: Just a glass of water would be lovely.

YLLI: You sure – a glass of juice or something? I have this –
  been saving – this is real Albanian drink – Rakia.

VIV: Is that a brandy?

YLLI: Yes it is – made from grapes – you can taste the soil,
  believe me.

VIV: Goodness.

YLLI: But we serve in hot tea tonight. Hot tea with brandy.

VIV: Well –

YLLI: Believe me, Viv, I'm not joking – in my country we
  serve this to our guests. Try it. Try it and tell me. I make
  subtle.

VIV: OK then – I'm up for anything!

  VIV laughs.

YLLI: Great, Viv, great!

BESNIK: I'll make it, Dad.

  BESNIK takes the bottle from YLLI and goes off to the kitchen.

YLLI: One for all of us, yes? It's a celebration. Neighbours
  together. At last.

VIV: I know – I can't believe we're in February. // Time just
  flies –

YLLI: Please, please, take a seat. No no not there, Viv – I'm
  sorry – there is a collapse there – you will fall through. Sit
  at –

VIV: I'll go at the end –

YLLI: Yes, and Ben – you go the other side.

BEN: Sure.

YLLI: *(Out of breath now and sweating with social excitement.)* And I here.

A moment as they all catch their breath.

VIV: So –

YLLI: Yes, Viv?

VIV: What's the rent these days for the council. Just out of interest.

YLLI: For this place. Too much. Believe me, oh my gosh!

VIV: Five hundred?

YLLI: Five hundred! No way. Not for this place. Can you imagine? They're sharks Viv, but they're not that bad. No, I pay two hundred and forty.

VIV: Two forty a month?

YLLI: Correct.

VIV is stunned.

YLLI: But of course I do everything else. The upkeep they never do. My friend did the floor – you see the floor – nice wooden floor.

BEN: Yeah, it's really nice.

YLLI: I got special rate. I can give you his number if you like?

Beat. VIV is looking at the floor.

BEN: Mum?

VIV: Yes? Thank you.

YLLI: No problem, Viv, no problem. *(Calling out.)* Besnik? How's the tea coming along? *(To VIV.)* My son is a perfectionist in everything he does. Can't think where he get's it from! So Viv, please, tell me. What do you think of my art?

VIV for the first time takes in the painting adorning the walls: big expressive landscapes and portraits. They are brilliant – and completely lost on VIV.

VIV: Wow. Did you do all of these?

YLLI: Of course, it's all my work.

BEN: They're amazing, Ylli.

YLLI: Thank you so much.

VIV: I like the tiger. Very colourful.

YLLI: *(Disappointed.)* That's your favourite?

VIV: Well I like all of them. They're all very different, aren't they?

YLLI: That one was from a photo, to be honest with you. To practice. Remember I say I'm still searching for my style?

BEN is looking at a large canvas depicting a stormy sea. A lone boat with a red sail is caught in the swirling mass.

BEN: This one of the storm is amazing.

YLLI: You like this one Viv?

VIV: *(Getting a good look.)* Oh yes – that's very dramatic, isn't it.

YLLI: Would it surprise you to learn that this is my self-portrait?

VIV: Self-portrait? Am I missing something!

YLLI: It's me, here. Not my face, but me.

BEN: You're the boat.

YLLI: That's right. There are waves around me, and rocks –
it's not good – but still I go.

BEN: I get it.

VIV: I like the red.

YLLI: The red is my flag. And it represents blood. We have
shed a lot of blood, as a nation.

They stare at it for a bit.

VIV: And did you train?

YLLI: Of course.

VIV: Oh yes you can tell. You can tell.

YLLI: I went to the Academy of Fine Arts, in Pristina, in
Kosovo. It was a very strict criteria to get in. You had to
demonstrate your skill in painting, drawing and sculpture
to three professors. If you weren't good, you wouldn't get
it. Don't forget, it was a communist country, so when it
came to art, music and literature, they were very strict.
High standards.

VIV: Well you think of all the great dancers – Rudolf Nureyev –

BESNIK comes in with a tray of tea. He serves it.

YLLI: And on my interview, I remember there was a line
of us, and we were all doing a live drawing. And the
professor – this big bald man with big ears – came up
close to me. He asked my name. I said it. He said, put
your pencil down and go home.

BEN: Oh no.

YLLI: I was very disappointed to be honest with you. I thought
I fucked up. But I was admitted.

BEN: Great!

YLLI: But I was very angry. I thought I fucked up –

BESNIK: *(Passing YLLI his cup.)* Dad.

VIV: But it was a happy ending! Good –

YLLI: No. The truth is I didn't finish my studies. I was there only two years and then the school got closed down. And not just mine but many institutions. The Serbs closed down everything. You must understand, Viv, they were scared of us, our potential, of what we might become. They even changed the school curriculum, made our children learn Serbian instead of Albanian – even the textbooks were changed to Serbian. Besnik – do you remember – he would come home with homework crying as he did not understand the questions – remember, Besnik?

BESNIK: Chocolate seashell, anyone?

BEN: Yes please.

VIV: I'll wait till after.

YLLI: You prefer cookie?

VIV: Honestly, I'm fine.

YLLI: That was one of the reasons we come here to be honest with you. They fucked my generation, but they would not fuck with my son's. Excuse my language, Viv.

VIV: Education is so important. My mother always said that.

YLLI: Clever lady, your mother.

BESNIK: Cheers everyone –

YLLI: Let me be host in my own house Besnik. Now everyone *(raising his cup)* as they say in my country: Gëzuar!

EVERYONE: Gëzuar!

They all drink.

VIV: Mmm. *(Feeling the effect of the brandy.)* So, why this country? What made you come here?

YLLI: I don't know. Why we chose. We just chose. People chose United States or Germany or whatever.

VIV: Because there does seem to be a lot of refugees coming here. And I'm all for that – of course I want everyone to be safe – but I just wonder if there's enough space? We're such a small country after all.

BEN: Of course there's space Mum.

YLLI: There is too many, I think, now. We're all competing for work. It's tough, now. Believe me. But what else can my people do?

Beat.

VIV: Frida Kahlo. That's who I'm mad about. Frida Kahlo? You know, talking about self-portraits. Her use of colour – all those pinks and reds – and the way she dressed. Oh she was wonderful – in everything... well I'm not mad about the skeletons, but she did what she wanted and I guess that's what an artist does, isn't it. They do it their own way. *(Taking another sip.)* And she was a fighter – despite that awful accident on the bus and all the other crap, she just filled her life with colour. No, she cheers me up. An inspiration.

YLLI: Frida Kahlo. Not bad – for a woman –

BESNIK: Dad –

YLLI: What – she was not trained. But she was talented. Of that I am sure.

VIV: Exactly. You have to be. To do what you do. You've got to be very good at sitting still, don't you? Thinking. Seeing

65

the images – no no, it's so clever. I can't imagine ever
having the time –

YLLI: There is never enough time –

VIV: But you have to stick at it. You never know who might
pass one of your paintings one day and go "Yes that's it"
– life can change in an instant like that. It's all timing –
everything is timing.

YLLI: And your painter friend – the one who did your
portrait? Perhaps he would like my work, Viv.

VIV: Robert? Oh gosh I lost touch with him years ago.
Wouldn't have a clue what he's doing now.

YLLI: But you can find out for me, maybe?

VIV: I don't know how…

BEN: I'm sure we can find out.

VIV: Well it's very difficult…

YLLI: But you're still in artist circles?

VIV: No. The circles change and… well it becomes hard
when you're a single mum – to reconnect. People who
you thought were your friends aren't. *(Sipping her tea.)*
Anyway. Ben can paint.

BEN: I can?

YLLI: You know, Viv, I would love to paint your son.

VIV: Oh yes do!

YLLI: I must, for he has a classical face. Very special.

VIV: He looks like my father.

YLLI: And of course, I won't charge you more than one fifty.
One hundred and fifty, that's it.

BESNIK: Dad.

VIV: I won't be able to afford that, I'm afraid.

YLLI: No? One fifty. In real price it would be five hundred.

BESNIK: Dad! I'm sorry Viv.

VIV: One day. One day you can paint him.

Beat.

YLLI: Forgive me, Viv, I hope I have not offend you.

VIV: No no.

YLLI: The truth is Viv, I'm struggling very much. I lost my job last month.

VIV: Oh no, what happened?

YLLI: They treated me very bad.

BESNIK: But you got some interviews coming up, and it's OK.

YLLI: I want to make money again from painting.

VIV: Why don't you take some of your work into galleries? See what they say.

YLLI: I had work in galleries once – here, Viv, in Whitechapel.

VIV: Did you? Well done.

YLLI: But they don't want me now. I need a way in.

VIV: I wish I could help.

Beat.

YLLI: You don't know anyone?

BESNIK: Dad, can you help me dish up?

67

YLLI: I can do portraits like yours for a good price.

VIV: I can definitely ask people.

YLLI: *(Pleased with this.)* Thank you. Thank you, Viv. If I have connection, then it will happen. I know this. I need just one connection, Viv, just one. Just one second yeah –

YLLI and BESNIK go into the kitchen.

VIV: We don't have to stay long.

BEN: Is there not anyone you know?

VIV: Do you smell pot?

BEN: Mum!

VIV: I'm going to make an excuse that we have to leave early.

BEN: Can you not be rude to them.

VIV: I'm not. But I'm feeling a bit pressured.

BEN: Is there no way we can help him?

VIV: With what? He's better off than we are. Two bedrooms –

BEN: Mum –

VIV: Why couldn't Jenny put us in one of these?

BEN: Because it's owned by the council.

VIV: It's not fair.

BEN: Mum – they've lost everything.

VIV: Well so have we!

YLLI comes in holding a large saucepan. BESNIK carries a tray with bowls.

YLLI: Dinner is ready. Stew.

VIV: Smells wonderful.

YLLI: My mother's recipe.

VIV: What's in it?

YLLI: Veal.

VIV: Veal?

BEN: Nice!

YLLI: *(Serving as he's talking.)* Not beef. Never beef. I don't like beef –

VIV: Just a little for me – that's lovely. Thank you.

BESNIK: You don't have to eat it all.

BESNIK passes VIV her bowl.

YLLI: And red pepper – how you say – paprika. Paprika –

VIV: *(Having a spoonful.)* Oh – hot hot hot.

BEN: Slow down Mum –

BESNIK: You OK?

YLLI: Onions – I use red ones – but you can use whatever you like –

VIV: *(Taking a sip of water.)* Ginger? I can taste the ginger.

YLLI: No – no ginger.

BESNIK passes BEN's bowl.

BESNIK: This OK?

BEN: Great. I'm starving. Thank you.

YLLI: Potatoes – chopped up. Like cubes.

VIV: Right.

YLLI: But first – and this is very important – first you must boil the meat for two hours in water. Only in water.

VIV: Right – not one to do in a rush!

YLLI: No no no no. Rushing not good. Take time. I don't like rushing. For everything, rushing not good. If you rush, you're going to damage.

VIV: It's very tender.

YLLI: And after two hours boiling the meat, you add the potatoes and onions and salt and paprika –

VIV: And peas, I see.

YLLI: Of course – but add in the last five minutes.

BESNIK: And that's it.

YLLI: Yes –

VIV: Wonderful. And so nice to have veal. One always forgets… veal.

YLLI: Eat, everyone, eat. Don't be shy.

YLLI takes big mouthfuls. They eat in silence for a bit.

BEN: It's delicious, thank you.

YLLI: You're welcome, Ben. I love this dish to be honest with you. I cook it all the time.

BESNIK gets up to turn the TV off.

YLLI: What are you doing?

BESNIK: We don't need this on.

YLLI: The Channel 4 News is about to start. Leave it.

BESNIK: Dad –

YLLI: Leave it. I need to know what's happening in my
country. Sorry, I understand it may be rude, but –

BEN: No no –

YLLI: But I have to follow. I have to.

YLLI eats while keeping one eye on the television.

VIV: That's alright. We actually can't stay that long. I have an
early meeting tomorrow –

YLLI: Ah yes. How are you finding your new job, Viv?

VIV: Love it. There was quite a lot to sort out when I arrived
but I'm slowly turning everything around. I think they're
all really pleased I'm there! The money's not great but
we'll see what happens…

VIV has lost YLLI. The Channel 4 News has begun.

VIV: And Besnik – tell me more about your course. When can
you be my accountant?

BESNIK: Summer if you like.

VIV: So soon?

BESNIK: I finish in May.

BEN: And he's already got a placement lined up.

VIV: A job?

BESNIK: Yes. I'm going to be a trainee accountant. In the City.

VIV: Wow. You must be very good.

BESNIK: I don't know about that.

BEN: You are – he is. He's really (---) good.

VIV: Lucky you. *(Looking at BEN and laughing.)* You were
bottom in your class for maths, weren't you?

BEN: Yeah.

VIV: What did your teacher say your report?
(To BESNIK.) Wait for it…

BEN: I couldn't do better if I tried.

VIV: *(Laughing.)* Oh darling *(playing with his head)* you'll get there in the end.

YLLI: *(In Albanian, at the TV.)* Fucking bastards.

They all look at the TV. Civilians lie on the ground, mutilated.

VIV: *(Turning away her gaze.)* Oh –

YLLI: You see what the Serbs are doing to our people?

BEN: How is that allowed on TV?

YLLI: Soon there'll be none of my people left. When will the world help us?

VIV: Is this really the thing to have on while we're eating?

BEN: Mum –

YLLI: Why aren't the weapons getting to the KLA? All that money, where's it going?

BESNIK: Dad –

YLLI: We need to have a chance to defend ourselves. Believe me. These Serbs will stop at nothing. It's in their blood to be like this. Murderers, rapists – animals! Not even animals could be so cruel –

BESNIK: I'm sorry guys –

YLLI: They don't have mercy. They don't care for human life. They are born like that. Vampires, sucking the blood –

BESNIK: Dad –

72

YLLI: They will never give up Kosovo. I know this. But it is our land, our country – not theirs.

BESNIK: *(In Albanian.)* Dad you're scaring them.

YLLI: *(Standing.)* Good! We should all be scared. This is genocide. Our people are being killed. They call it ethnic cleansing now. The West. But this war has been going on for long time. And still they wait, the West, they wait till nearly all our women and children are dead before the bombs come. Like they did with Bosnia. Assholes.

VIV: *(Getting up.)* Maybe this isn't a good time.

YLLI: No no – forgive me – don't go yet.

BEN: Mum, we're eating.

VIV: No I'm sorry I – I understand it's a stressful time and… but I can't look at this when I'm eating, I can't. You can stay if you want, Ben, but I'm…

BEN: *(Getting up.)* I'm really sorry.

BESNIK: It's OK.

VIV: Let's wait till everything calms down. Yes? Then we can make a plan.

YLLI: Wait? I can't wait anymore. I'm going over to fight.

BEN: Fight where?

YLLI: In my country – yes Ben!

BESNIK: *(In Albanian.)* Dad, sit down.

YLLI: I've decided Besnik. I'm going over to fight. I can't sit by and watch this anymore. I have to go.

BESNIK looks away.

73

(In Albanian, excited.) Come with me, son. If we die fighting for our country so be it. We will die as heroes. You and me.

VIV: What's he saying? What's he talking about?

YLLI throws his arms up to the heavens.

YLLI: Our destiny!

Blackout.

SCENE EIGHT

The next week, premature sign of spring outside – light is getting through Viv's curtains.

VIV's flat.

BEN playing, BESNIK watching.

BESNIK: So now we have to get the Triforce.

BEN: Correct.

BESNIK: I don't understand. What is that?

BEN: It's the scale that measures the three virtues: Power, Courage and Wisdom.

BESNIK: In that order?

BEN: In any order. That's what came to mind.

BESNIK: Why do we need it?

BEN: Because whoever finds it has to be balanced in all three. The worry is that Ganondorf will get their first, and that he will destroy Hyrule with his power – because power is his only virtue.

BESNIK: Whereas we…

BEN: Whereas Link is balanced in all three. I think. I guess that's what we're going to find out.

BESNIK: So why aren't you heading to the castle?

BEN: I want to find all the fairies first.

BESNIK: What would you say your main virtue is?

BEN: Out of those three?

BESNIK: Yes.

BEN: Maybe... no

BESNIK: No go on – what were you going to say?

BEN: Maybe wisdom?

BESNIK laughs.

BEN: Oh OK. Maybe not. I don't know. I don't have one. I'm not like you.

BESNIK: Oh wait, so what do I have?

BEN: Power.

BESNIK: Damn right I got power.

BEN: Yeah. You do. You're very powerful. Your... presence.

BESNIK looks at him.

BEN: What?

I don't know, I'm just saying... I don't know you.

Stop it! You're putting me off!

BESNIK keeps on staring at him – he's enjoying it.

Stop!

BEN dies.

Fuck! I've died.

Happy now?

Do you want a go?

BESNIK kisses BEN.

A very long moment.

BESNIK picks up the controller.

BESNIK: Sure.

I think yours might be courage.

BEN is confused and doesn't know what to do. He watches the screen for a bit, before summoning his courage.

BEN: Me too.

BEN kisses BESNIK. The lights fade as they catch up for lost time. Mariah Carey sings.

SCENE NINE

March 11th 1999.

This scene is split between VIV's and YLLI's bedrooms.

In VIV's room: VIV, in her dressing gown, is sat at her dressing table blow-drying her hair. BEN is on her bed, made to look smart in shirt and trousers.

In YLLI's: YLLI, in his vest and shorts, is having a wet shave over the sink. His suit is laid out next to him. BESNIK is sat on the bed, watching.

VIV: *(Stopping her hairdryer and brushing her hair.)* Penny.

BEN: What?

VIV: Penny. For your thoughts.

BEN: Not much.

BESNIK: And what do you do when you get there?

YLLI: I have an interview.

BESNIK: With who?

YLLI: Some KLA representative.

VIV: I can always tell when something is bothering you.

BEN: Nothing's bothering me. I just don't know why he can't come here for dinner that's all.

VIV: He wants to spoil us.

YLLI: They will ask me questions. And then I will take an oath in front of our flag that I will fight till the end for the freedom of my country.

BESNIK: And then?

YLLI: And then I wait and see, Besnik.

VIV: We're going to the theatre and then to The Ivy afterwards. I can't remember last time I was at The Ivy. I used to go there with your dad quite a lot.

BEN: So you tell me a million times.

VIV: What's wrong?

NIK: It's illegal.

YLLI: Illegal? There's nothing illegal about the Kosovo Liberation Army, believe me.

BESNIK: Right. Apart from the fact that it's financed by drug money. It's no secret now, Dad. They're being called terrorists in the press.

BEN: I know you don't fancy him.

VIV: You have no idea how my heart works.

BEN: I know when it lies.

YLLI: We've been called terrorists for years, Besnik. Serbian propaganda to create fear. It's how they've kept us down for so long.

BESNIK: They have enough fighters, Dad. They don't need more.

YLLI: I understand where you stand on this Besnik. I don't agree, but I understand.

VIV: He's not like the others. He's got a real sense of humour.

BEN: Can't wait for that.

VIV: And I'm just me when I'm with him. I'm not anyone else.

YLLI: I want you to come with me.

BESNIK: No, papa.

YLLI: But what will happen if I go? What will you do?

BESNIK: I'll survive.

YLLI: I always thought you would change your mind.

VIV: Everyone deserves love sweetheart.

BEN: You never needed it before.

VIV: Ben –

BEN: Fucking hell. Are you that sick of me? To throw yourself at the first man to buy you dinner. What's wrong with you?

VIV: Don't you dare to speak to me like that. Don't you dare! You are still my son. Show me some fucking manners. You arsehole. You have no idea // what I've sacrificed for you –

BEN: Oh yes, tell me again, how much you *sacrificed for me.* // Please – I haven't heard it enough – how you paid for my education, how Dad's done nothing –

VIV: Stop it Ben –

BEN: I never asked for any of it. It was your decision –

VIV: I've always wanted us to be happy –

BEN: You just want yourself to be happy. And I've been tagging along with you, all this time, as you chase your, your (---) fucking happiness.

BESNIK: We came to this country to escape war, not to go back to it.

YLLI: You don't understand, I was weak back then –

BESNIK: No –

VIV: Is that what you think?

YLLI: Your mother, I loved your mother, but she pushed me to leave and I listened to her.

BESNIK: Because of what happened to us!

YLLI: I never got to have my revenge.

BESNIK: But she rescued us, don't you understand, she rescued us. If she listened to you, we would have died!

Beat.

We would have died.

BESNIK covers his face to cry. BEN mirrors his pose.

VIV: *(Moving to BEN.)* Come on, darling. Don't cry. Please. Ben?

BEN: I emailed Dad.

VIV: Did you? What did he say?

BEN: He wants me to come to Malaysia. To hear his side of the story.

VIV: His side? Well you can go over and tell him my side. Face to face. If that's how he wants to play it. His side!

YLLI: Besnik. Besnik. Move your hand from your face. I want to see your tears.

BESNIK wipes his tears off.

Not all men were born to fight. But for some men, it is their destiny. You are a fighter in a different way. Maybe even in a better way, perhaps, I don't know. I can only try and understand. Now please understand me.

BEN: It doesn't matter now.

YLLI: Yes, Besnik?

BESNIK: Yes, papa.

YLLI washes his face. He puts on his clothes.

VIV: Of course it matters.

BEN: But you're moving on. And I'm… here.

VIV: With me.

BEN: You are not my life, Mum!

Beat.

VIV goes back to her dressing table. Something has broken inside. She sits, carrying on doing her make-up.

BEN: I do love you though. Mum? It doesn't mean I don't love you. Mum?

VIV: Let's not get heavy, Ben.

BEN: I'm not – I just want you to // understand

VIV: I'll tell Philip you were ill. OK? You can stay and play your game tonight.

BEN: Mum –

VIV: Leave me to get on with this in peace. Please, Ben, leave me alone just now.

A moment, then BEN leaves VIV alone. YLLI is now changed.

YLLI: We will have our country back. We will live as Albanians in Kosovo once more. You will be able to start a family and live a life of peace. More than I have had.

BESNIK: Good luck, Papa.

YLLI goes over, kisses BESNIK on the head and goes.

March 25th, 1999.

VIV's flat.

BEN playing, his brow more furrowed than usual. BESNIK comes in like a newly popped bottle of champagne. He is wearing VIV's dressing gown.

BESNIK: Is this silk?

BEN: Yeah. It was from her range. Didn't take off.

BESNIK: Why not? I feel a million dollars.

BESNIK does a catwalk down the room in front of BEN.

BEN: Stop – I can't see.

BESNIK: Can you fuck me wearing this?

BEN: Take it off now.

BESNIK: You take it off.

BEN: No – I'm nearly at the castle dungeon.

BESNIK: We've had sex three times today and your head was on that castle dungeon, wasn't it?

BEN: No.

BESNIK: That's OK. I was kind of thinking about Doritos. Do you have any?

BEN: No. I need to go for the shop for Mum.

BESNIK: Actually jizz will be really hard to get off this. Oh my God, do you think she wears this while fucking that Philip?

BEN: Besnik!

BESNIK: *(Impersonating Philip having sex.)* Oh yeah, spank my bottom, Viv, spank it – make it feel good –

BEN: I'm going to throw this at you.

BESNIK: No you're not.

BESNIK: Can we go out?

BEN: I need to finish this.

BESNIK: No don't rush the ending. Let's go out. It's sunny.

BEN: OK. But not the park.

BESNIK: You only like dark places, don't you. Alright, let's go to Old Compton Street.

BEN looks at BESNIK.

BESNIK: That got your attention.

BEN: Isn't that in Soho?

BESNIK: It's really fun.

BEN: …

BESNIK: Don't freak out! It's fine. There are loads of bars we can go to. Places to dance. It's cool. We could have a good time.

BEN doesn't know what to say.

BESNIK: Breathe Ben.

BEN: Have you been?

BESNIK: Yes.

BEN: How often have you been?

BESNIK: A few times.

BEN: ...

BESNIK: You know the night I got locked out?

BEN: Yeah.

BESNIK: I went that night.

BEN: But you got beaten up!

BESNIK: Not from the gays!

BEN: Who from then?

BESNIK: From – why does that matter?

BEN focuses back on the game.

BESNIK: Why has this freaked you out?

BEN: It hasn't, I just thought you were happy doing this.

BESNIK: I am.

BEN: But... you want to go and meet other people.

BESNIK looks at him.

BEN: I don't.

BESNIK: Why do you think I want to meet other people?

BEN: Because you're bored with me.

BESNIK: Is that what you honestly think?

BEN: I don't want to keep you prisoner. You go if you want to.

BESNIK: Ben! I've been sucking your cock // all morning –

BEN: Shhss!

BESNIK: What?

BEN: Is your dad not...

84

BESNIK: He's at work.

BEN: He's found a job?

BESNIK: No he's... training

BESNIK's mood changes. He takes off VIV's dressing gown.

BEN: For what?

BESNIK: CCTV.

BEN: Oh right. That's good.

BESNIK starts changing back into his clothes.

BEN: I saw that NATO has decided to bomb Serbia. That's good, isn't it.

BESNIK: Since when was bombing good?

BEN: They're the bad guys.

BESNIK: Who are they? The Serbian people?

BEN: Yeah... well the ones that want to kill your people.

BESNIK: So you think blood can only be wiped out with blood?

BEN: No.

BESNIK: So surely bombing is not good.

BEN: I don't know.

BESNIK: Stop saying you don't know. You can't hide behind "I don't know." "I don't know" will not save you.

Beat.

BESNIK: I'm going to go.

BEN: OK. See you tomorrow?

BESNIK: I don't know.

BESNIK leaves. BEN carries on playing.

SCENE ELEVEN

The same. Later that day.

VIV and BEN are eating fish and chips on the sofa. There is lightness, a return to old times as the scene begins.

VIV: I think these are the best ones yet, don't you?

BEN: Yeah.

VIV: You've got colour back in your cheeks again. You must be feeling better.

BEN nods.

VIV: Do you remember that fish and chips we had in Cornwall?

BEN: The one where you got attacked by all the seagulls?

VIV: And you told me to run into the sea!

BEN: They were attacking you! They weren't stopping!

VIV: It was awful – and you were laughing!

BEN: I didn't think you'd actually do it –

VIV: I was terrified!

BEN: You're insane.

They laugh.

VIV: Oh we've had some adventures, haven't we. Since you were two we've been on the road, finding our home.

BEN: Yeah.

VIV puts her fish and chips down.

BEN: Are you alright?

VIV: Philip's asked if we'd like to move in with him.

BEN: OK.

VIV: And I've said yes.

A moment.

VIV: I know it may seem sudden. But I love him.

I've been thinking a lot about what you said, about living your own life, and I do want that for you.

BEN: I know –

VIV: And this way, moving in with Philip will give you that freedom. You can have your own space for once. I mean it's huge, this house, it's in Richmond, it's – it's in a good area – safe. And your room is at the top – it's out the way – you won't even notice us – you can do what you like up there and... and just kick on with being you, sweetheart.

BEN stares into his fish and chips.

VIV: And we can still have our fish and chips on Friday nights, and we can still go to the cinema – it can all be the same – if you want that, darling.

It will be a proper home for us.

BEN: This is home.

VIV: Let's be honest, it's been stressful and difficult –

BEN: I'm not moving.

VIV: It won't be until May.

87

BEN: I don't care, Mum, I'm not. I'm not doing it anymore. Sorry.

VIV: Ben –

BEN: You can tell Philip thanks but I'd rather live on my own –

VIV: I'd thought you'd be pleased, I –

BEN: Don't I have a say?

VIV: Of course you do –

BEN: Well I'm not moving with him. Sorry.

VIV: So where are you going to go then?

BEN: …

VIV: You don't want to live with us, fine, but where are you going to stay?

BEN: I'll find somewhere, Mum, OK-

VIV: Well it can't be with your father, so where?

BEN: I need time to think about it.

VIV: How are you going to pay for your rent? I'm just wondering, sweetheart, because you don't have a job // and you'll need an income to support yourself

BEN: I know I don't have a job –

VIV: How are you going to do it then? How are you going to be in the world if you don't engage with it? Life doesn't just happen, you have to work for it, you have to fight for it.

BEN: Well I'll start fighting now then.

VIV: But you can't. You can't start with nothing!

BEN: I'm not nothing. I've got… I've got stuff in me… I've got stuff that I can… do…

VIV: Oh look –

BEN: No don't patronise me –

VIV: I'm not –

BEN: You are –

VIV: It's just you have no idea what it's really like. And maybe that's my fault. I've protected you too much from the reality of life –

BEN: Are you serious?

VIV: And as a result I've raised a son who can't even hand in his CV to a nursery school without having a fucking panic attack. Jesus Christ – you're nearly twenty –

BEN: Shut up!

VIV: *(Fearful, yelling.)* What are you going to do Ben? What are you going to do? If you don't want to live with me, fine, but I need to know that you are going to be OK.

Beat. BEN can't find the reassurance. VIV waves away her emotion.

VIV: I'm sorry. I'm getting heavy. Let's talk about something else – yes? *(Picking up her fish and chips.)* Do you want the rest of my chips?

BEN shakes his head.

VIV: They are big portions.

VIV casts her eye around the flat.

VIV: In a funny way, I've grown quite fond of this place. Bit like going to the hairdressers, isn't it; always looks best before it's cut.

A long moment. A fighter jet flies by overhead, loud.

89

VIV: And it'll be nice to move away from them, won't it darling. Although, I feel you've enjoyed having someone to talk to, in Besnik, haven't you?

BEN: Yeah.

VIV: Anyway, more importantly, what game do you want for your birthday?

SCENE TWELVE

April 30ᵗʰ 1999.

Outside a pub in Soho.

Late afternoon. A hot night for April. Revellers are starting to take their drinks outside. BEN and BESNIK are holding their pints.

BESNIK: I've got to say, I much prefer twenty-year-old Ben.

BEN: Same. Nineteen-year-old Ben was a twat.

BESNIK: Major twat. Major wet twat.

BEN: Yeah – so wet, so fucking wet.

BESNIK: Like, dripping –

BEN: Gushing – into a massive hole of… wetness.

BESNIK: But twenty-year-old Ben – he saved the day.

BEN: He did.

BEN does another glance around.

BESNIK: She's not going to be here.

BEN: Who?

BESNIK: Your mum.

BEN: Oh yes – I know. Philip's helping her pack today.

BESNIK: He's keen.

BEN: I think he's lonely.

BESNIK: Shame. I was hoping to watch the eclipse with you on the roof.

BEN: We can still do that. Can't we?

BESNIK: Not if you're not a tenant...

BEN looks worried.

BESNIK: Course you can. So you think Jane's got another move in her?

BEN: Mum's going to put her down.

BESNIK: What? No!

BEN: She's getting really rank now. She keeps peeing.

BESNIK: That's no reason to kill her!

BEN: She's really old.

BESNIK: I don't care! No one is killing me off, no matter how rank I get. People can just shovel my shit till the end.

BEN: Are you scared of death?

BESNIK: Not the old age kind. But by other people, yes.

BEN: By other people?

BESNIK: Yeah – dickheads – getting in your way. Cutting your life short by stress. Other people are nightmares. Not you though. You're a nightmare to yourself.

BEN: Not by choice.

BESNIK: Of course by choice.

BEN: I'm scared of ruining my life.

91

BESNIK: You're scared of standing here.

BEN: Well yeah, life's scary. It's all so… much.

BESNIK kisses BEN

BESNIK: You scared now?

BEN: No. I feel (---) good.

BESNIK: What were you going to say?

BEN: I feel safe with you.

Beat.

BEN: Sorry – that's not really sexy is it. I also really love your ass – and your face –

BESNIK: I want you to move in with me.

Beat.

BEN: Where?

BESNIK: Into my flat! I don't want you going with your mum. I want you to move in with me.

BEN: But your Dad –

BESNIK: He's not there.

BEN: Where is he?

BESNIK: He's gone back to Kosovo, to fight.

BEN: What –

BESNIK: You can't tell anyone.

BEN: Jesus –

BESNIK: Ben – you can't tell anyone.

BEN: No I won't, I… wow.

BESNIK: So what do you think?

BEN: It's just a lot of information.

BESNIK: We can do this. It's legal. Twenty, Ben!

BEN: But I – I haven't got a job.

BESNIK: I'll help you get a job. There's no reason you can't get a job –

BEN: No you don't understand – I tried –

BESNIK: There's no reason.

BEN: What do I say to my mum? I can't tell her that... I'm – I'll be telling her then about me. About...

BESNIK: You don't have to tell her anything if you don't want to.

BEN: I've got to say something.

BESNIK: Say you want to be a grown-up. And you can't do that living with her.

BEN: I kind of said that already but – I can't just leave her.

BESNIK: She has Philip now.

BEN: ...

BESNIK: We can have so much fun together. We can live the way we want to. Like everyone else here! Don't you want to be free?

BEN: I am sort of free.

BESNIK: Ben – come on – there is nothing stopping us – nothing stopping you. We're a team.

Beat. BEN takes in the street, the people, the colours. He inhales the freedom.

BEN: *(Breathing out.)* Woah.

93

BESNIK: Are you OK?

BEN: Yeah – yeah I am. Twenty. *(BEN finishes his drink.)* I think I need another.

BESNIK: I think so too. I'll get these.

BESNIK takes the empty pint glasses.

BESNIK: Try not to run away with anyone.

BESNIK smiles and goes inside. BEN feels the warmth in his heart overcome him. He looks to the sky. A cloud goes over the sun, and then the street bursts into flames.

Blackout.

SCENE THIRTEEN

That evening. YLLI's flat.

YLLI has just come in. Dishevelled with the smell of alcohol on his breath, he is holding a bag with an airline sticker on it. He takes in the clean flat.

YLLI: Besnik?

No answer. YLLI drops his bag and heads over to the drinks cabinet. He takes out a bottle of Rakia, and has a swig.

YLLI: Besnik? Where are you Besnik…

Taking another swig, YLLI goes over to the TV, puts it on and crashes down on the sofa.

A knock on the door.

YLLI: Yes?

VIV: *(Off.)* It's Viv from next door.

YLLI: *(Jumping up.)* I'm coming Viv, I'm coming, just a second, huh –

YLLI opens the door. VIV comes in, anxious.

VIV: He's not in?

YLLI: Hello Viv – how are you –

VIV: Ben? He's not here?

YLLI: Ben? No, no one is here. I am alone.

VIV: Right. OK. Sorry – I – I haven't seen him all day and he was meant to be helping me pack. I –

YLLI: Take a seat, Viv, take a seat.

VIV sits down and stands up again.

VIV: Sorry – he's not with Besnik?

YLLI: My son is an enigma to me, Viv. I cannot know where he is or even who he is, for that matter – excuse me – *(Belching into his hand.)* Can I get you a drink?

VIV: No – I can't stay – I – I –

YLLI: You need to sit down and relax. Please sit.

VIV gives up and sits. YLLI pours her a drink.

VIV: I know he's probably fine and I'm being crazy –

YLLI: Ben? He has a classical face, your son, and he is young. He will be fine, believe me, fine. *(Handing VIV a drink.)* Here, this will settle you.

VIV: Thank you.

YLLI: If he's anything like my boy, you should be grateful he doesn't tell you where he's going. Believe me. It's not our business. You understand me? I think you do. I think you do, Viv. Yes – I always knew they would be friends.

95

VIV: He's never been sociable before. It's always been like pulling teeth to get him… out the house, let alone…

YLLI: Young people are like sand, you can't hold them – they'll find a way out.

VIV: No, that's true.

YLLI: It's always true. No exception. Believe me.

Beat. VIV struggles to contain her worry.

VIV: Sorry – I – do you know when you have a sixth sense?

YLLI: Sixth sense – like the movie – seeing ghosts?

VIV: No not like that – it's more – a feeling that something's wrong. A feeling in here and – and I've had it before with him and… I've always been right. I've always been right to worry.

YLLI refills his glass.

YLLI: It's not easy raising a son on your own, I know.

VIV: No, it's not that. It's just he's been very up and down recently…

YLLI takes out a cigarette from his box of Camel Blues. He offers one to VIV.

VIV: No thanks.

YLLI: Come on, Viv.

VIV hesitates before taking one.

YLLI: Sometimes we need. We need it, Viv. This life, this time, it's not good. Not good at all, believe me.

They light up. VIV relaxes a bit.

VIV: But that's just it. Everything is good. For the first time in a long time I feel all the pieces of the jigsaw are finally falling into place. Life is finally giving back but... I just wish we could all be happy at the same time.

YLLI laughs.

YLLI: That's naïve.

VIV: I'm not naïve. It's taken me a lot of work to get where I am. To push through the crap. To not be defeated. When I feel the bad feelings beginning to take root, I move. I just move. I move on. Because if I don't... there's been a lot of sad people in my life. And I can't afford to be another one. It would be too unfair. For Ben and – well for me actually.

Beat. Stillness permeates the room.

VIV: Sorry, I haven't come here to offload... but I do wonder if he had more of a stable, I don't know, presence in his life... then maybe he wouldn't be so... I don't know.

YLLI: You don't know. None of us know. We have to make peace with that.

VIV: They grow up so quickly and before you know it, you've fucked them up.

YLLI laughs.

YLLI: But out of love, Viv, always out of love.

VIV: How have you found it?

YLLI: I am not enough for my son, and I accept that. He has outgrown me. He is like his mother, who was very wise, Viv, very wise. She was a professor – can you imagine – in my country, before we left. Maths. Very clever. I was the fire and she was the air – that's why we worked as a team. And when she died the balance was broken and my son had to grow up. But he has enough of her wisdom and also enough of my fire. I don't worry about him.

VIV: You don't? How do you not?

YLLI: Trust, Viv. Trust.

Beat. VIV for the first time understands YLLI.

VIV: What happened to her?

YLLI: Breast cancer. Two years after we arrived here. Like that. Gone.

VIV: I'm sorry.

YLLI: At thirty-six. Too young. It was the trauma that gave her cancer. I know this. Nobody can hold all that pain without the body wanting to find a way to die. It was heartbreak for me, Viv. I will never get over it. Never.

A long silence. Somewhere a clock in the room strikes ten. On TV the news begins. We see footage of a bombed building.

YLLI: NATO is really hammering Belgrade now. Look.

VIV: That's not Serbia. That's here.

YLLI turns up the TV.

NEWS JOURNALIST: Yes I can confirm that a nail bomb went off at the Admiral Duncan pub here in Soho at 6:30. Eyewitnesses report hearing a loud explosion, like a clap of thunder, then seeing individuals thrown thirty feet in the air –

VIV: Jesus!

YLLI: This is London?

VIV: I can't hear –

The door opens, and BESNIK enters unseen. He has blood on his torn clothes. He watches them watch the news. He is calling Papa but no sound is coming out.

Blackout.

SCENE FOURTEEN

May. Two weeks later.

VIV's flat.

Midday. The sun is shining brightly through the now empty flat. The windows are open. A soft breeze is gently blowing VIV's curtains – the only thing left – around. Soft reggae music is heard outside, laughter, the smell of barbecues…

VIV and BESNIK are stood. There is no trace of the attack on BESNIK's body, but the rigour in which he held himself before is gone.

VIV: Was it his idea to go?

BESNIK: No. It was mine.

VIV: Did you persuade him? Did he not want to go?

BESNIK: He wanted to go, but he was scared about it.

VIV: And you pushed him anyway.

BESNIK: He was happy when he was there. I promise you. He was happy.

VIV: Do you think he's happy now?

Beat.

BESNIK: I will never forgive myself.

VIV: Look that's not what I'm asking you to say –

BESNIK: But I will look after him for the rest of my life // I promise you

VIV: Oh no no – you are not going anywhere near my son.

BESNIK: Viv.

VIV: You are never seeing him again. Ever. Do you understand? I trusted you. I put my trust in you as our neighbour and you destroyed that. You have destroyed my son's life.

BESNIK: I didn't –

VIV: You did! If he hadn't gone with you to that place – and he wouldn't have done, on his own, he wouldn't have done – he would have just stayed in here, safe, playing his fucking game.

VIV put's her head in her hands.

He would still be here with me now, carrying on as if nothing had happened. And now everything has happened. Can you see that? Can you?

BESNIK: Yes. And it's not fair. It makes no sense. I don't understand.

VIV: Well I need to understand. I need to understand what you were doing with him.

BESNIK: We were just being with each other.

VIV: You were trying to make him something he wasn't.

BESNIK: No, I was letting him be himself. We were just being ourselves.

VIV: But he's always been himself. He can't help but be himself. I know my son. He could barely leave the flat to get milk and I'm meant to believe he was wanting to go and... it's not him, he's never shown the slightest... interest...

VIV starts to see that's not true.

VIV: Oh why did we ever move here? This is all my fault, this is all my fault, this is all my fault –

BESNIK: No –

VIV: I thought coming back to London – coming back to where I used to be – would help, would free us. But I just put him into another prison, another dark prison and I can't join him there. I can't let him see that it's OK.

VIV sits on the ground, sobbing.

I'm sorry. Oh God. Help me, someone please. I can't do it anymore. I can't – I just can't.

BESNIK sits next to her. He lets her cry.

BESNIK: This is not your fault. What happened was crazy and unimaginable and nothing to do with us. I wish I could be in Ben's place but I can't. I wish I could kill the man who did this but I can't. I wish we could protect the ones we love, but we can't.

VIV: No but I could have – I could have –

BESNIK: No you couldn't have. When I was ten, Serbian policeman broke into our house and tortured us. One by one. In front of each other. I couldn't do anything to protect my mum, my dad or myself. It happened. We all wished we could have done more, and I've seen that wish destroy both my parents.

VIV: He was my responsibility – he was my boy. He was my boy!

BESNIK: He's an adult, Viv. And he was living his life that day. Happy.

VIV: Happy!

BESNIK: Yes! He felt free for the first time. And he was with someone who… who loves him. And we were celebrating ourselves. And I'm sorry there was someone else there who didn't like that. But that person is not my fault, not Ben's fault and it definitely isn't yours.

VIV: But then why didn't he tell me this was how he felt? I would have listened. I would have tried to have helped in some way. I only ever wanted to help him.

Beat.

So what do we do now?

BESNIK: I want him to live with me.

VIV: No.

BESNIK: We made a plan – together – before… I love him, Viv. I love him. I don't care about what's happened to him. I want to be there for him, always.

VIV: He is not ready for that.

BESNIK: He is.

VIV: He's coming to live with me and Philip.

BESNIK: He won't want that.

VIV: How do you know?

BESNIK: Let me see him.

VIV: I don't know if that's a good idea. He's still in shock.

BESNIK: I understand all about shock.

VIV: But this is different –

BESNIK: How?

VIV: I'm sorry, I can't trust you with him.

BESNIK: Please Viv.

VIV: No. He's my son. Alright. I know what's best for him. You've done enough. You have done enough.

Beat.

BESNIK: OK. I'm sorry. I'm so sorry. Will you at least tell him what I said?

VIV: I want you take that box.

BESNIK sees the box by the door.

BESNIK: What is it?

VIV: Ben's Nintendo. He doesn't need it now does he. And I certainly don't want to see it again...

BESNIK picks up the box.

BESNIK: We never completed it. Zelda. He wanted to finish it that day, but I said wait. It was such a nice day.

Beat.

BESNIK goes. VIV bursts into heavy sobs. To control herself, she goes about locking up the windows. As she closes the last window, the singing fish falls to the floor. It starts to sing 'Don't Worry, Be Happy'. She sits under the window crying as the singing fish serenades her.

SCENE FIFTEEN

August 11ᵗʰ, 1999.

10am.

A rooftop in the World's End estate.

BESNIK is laying out a makeshift rug. They are both in the their shorts and vests. Music is playing off their portable radio.

BEN: It's hot – the tarmac

BESNIK: Stand on the towel now – here.

> *BESNIK helps him onto the towel.*

BEN: Is this one of Mum's ponchos?

BESNIK: How did you know?

BEN: What else have you stolen from her wardrobe?

BESNIK: Just the essentials. Sit.

> *BEN sits.*

BEN: You sure this is legal?

BESNIK: No.

BEN: And we're not too near the edge are we?

BESNIK: We're right in the middle, don't worry.

BEN: Cool.

BESNIK: You go such a nice colour in the sun.

BEN: Do I?

BESNIK: Yeah. My lovely golden boy.

> *BESNIK kisses BEN's shoulder.*

BEN: How long have we got –

BESNIK: Hold on – I'm tuning into Patrick Moore – he'll tell us. I love Patrick Moore.

BESNIK finds the station; we hear the commentary faintly.

BEN: I love his voice.

BESNIK: Like he's from a different time, isn't it?

BEN: Wasn't he born in the last century?

BESNIK: Can't be that old!

BEN: Imagine if he is – he could see in his third century.

BESNIK: Let's hope the excitement of the eclipse doesn't do him in then.

BEN: Can I have my Coke now?

BESNIK: Alright bossy!

BESNIK passes BEN a Coke.

BEN: *(Opening his Coke.)* So apparently I might experience a bit of a shadow.

BESNIK: Oh yeah?

BEN: Yeah. Well that's something isn't it.

BESNIK: It's going to be better in Cornwall – the full eclipse.

BEN: Sorry – did you want to go to Cornwall?

BESNIK: Shut up. This is great. I'm happy.

BESNIK opens his Coke.

BEN: Can you tell me what's happening please?

BESNIK: Yes. Nothing's happening yet.

BEN: Really?

BESNIK: Hold on –

BESNIK puts on his solar eclipse protective sunglasses.

BEN: Are you putting on your glasses?

BESNIK: Yeah.

BEN: Cool.

BESNIK: *(Looking up to the sky.)* The moon is drawing in slowly.

BEN: Oh cool – is it weird?

BESNIK: Hold on – there's a cloud.

BEN: Oh. Does feel a bit cold actually.

BESNIK: You're so full of shit.

BEN: It does.

BESNIK gets out his camera. He takes a picture of them both.

BESNIK: That's going to be cute.

BEN: Picture?

BESNIK: Something for the grandkids.

BEN: Whose?

BESNIK: Fuck you.

BEN: It's cool your work have given you the morning off. Do you think everyone's got the morning off?

BESNIK: I called in sick.

BEN: Besnik!

BESNIK: OK – so it's getting a bit yellower.

BEN: Really!

BESNIK: Yeah! Like a kind of murky yellow.

BEN: Oh wow.

Beat.

BEN: And it's getting quiet. Listen.

London goes quiet.

BESNIK: Not even the birds.

BEN: Do you think they're like, what the fuck's happening?

BESNIK: No they know.

BEN: It's getting darker, isn't it?

BESNIK: Yeah, it's happening quite quickly now.

BEN: I can see it. I can see it!

BESNIK: Yeah?

BEN: Yes.

BEN finds BESNIK's hand.

BESNIK: What's that for?

BEN: I'm happy too.

The moon goes in front of the sun.

Fade to black.

End of play.

WWW.OBERONBOOKS.COM

Follow us on Twitter @oberonbooks
& Facebook @OberonBooksLondon